ISBN 978-1-331-81230-2
PIBN 10237940

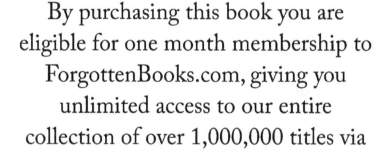

HONOR

A Play in Four Acts

BY
HERMANN SUDERMANN

TRANSLATED BY
HILMAR R. BAUKHAGE
WITH A PREFACE BY
BARRETT H. CLARK

NEW YORK
SAMUEL FRENCH
PUBLISHER
28-30 WEST 39TH STREET

LONDON
SAMUEL FRENCH, LTD.
26 SOUTHAMPTON STREET
STRAND

Wahr
8152
German
1-18-1923

HONOR

The French expression, a "man of the theater," is best exemplified in the person of the German dramatist Hermann Sudermann. The term is intended to convey the idea of a playwright who is interesting and effective, one who is, in short, master of his trade. The author of " Die Ehre," which is here presented for the first time to English readers, was for many years a man of the theater in the strictest acceptance of the term.

Hermann Sudermann was born at Matziken, Prussia, in 1857. After receiving his preliminary scholastic training in his native province, he attended the Universities of Konigsberg and Berlin and immediately after his graduation from the latter institution entered the field of journalism. His first works were short stories and novels, of which " Dame Care," " Regina," and " The Song of Songs " are the best known. German critics and the German reading public are inclined, of late years, in view of Sudermann's repeated failures in the field of drama, to place his fiction on a distinctly higher plane than his plays, and it is true that much of the finer intelligence of the man has gone to the making of his better novels. However, the earlier plays exerted an influence so widespread and are of such unquestioned intrinsic value, that there is some question as to the ultimate disposition of the laurels.

"Honor" was published in book form in 1888, the year before the founding of the famous "Freie Buhne," or "Free Theater," which was to usher in and nourish modern German Realism. It was first produced in 1890.

While Sudermann was not properly speaking a member of the new movement, his early works, "Honor" in particular, were shaped by and served partially to create the ideas which the founders of the "Freie Buhne," Arno Holz and Johannes Schlaf, had formulated. But a closer inspection of "Honor," of "The Destruction of Sodom," "Magda," and "The Joy of Living," leads us to the conclusion that Sudermann was playing with the Naturalistic formula, using it as a means rather than an end. One example will suffice: Arno Holz invented the phrase "Sequential Realism," by which he meant the chronological setting down of life in as minute and truthful a manner as possible. He aimed at the photographic reproduction of life; that process he called "art re-making nature." In his own plays, above all in "Die Familie Selicke," written in collaboration with Schlaf, his skill in noting details, his quest for truth at all costs, lent a decided air of actuality to the work, and the *appearance* was what Sudermann, who was more of an artist than the pair of young revolutionists, strove to imitate. After all, Sudermann is little more than a surface Realist, for he incorporated only what seemed to him valuable in the new formulas. Sudermann is the lineal descendant of Augier, Dumas fils and Sardou; he introduced into Germany a new manner of combining much that was good of the conventional and some that would prove beneficial of the Realistic ideas. The long speeches of Trast, the numerous asides, the more or less conventional exposition, the rather rhetorical style of the dialog, are reminiscent of the mid-century French dramatists, while the carefully observed types, the attention paid to detail, the occasionally realistic language, are indicative of the new spirit which was about to manifest itself in so concrete a form as the " Freie Buhne."

" Honor " is clearly a thesis play: it aims at the presentation and consideration of an idea, a problem, and the problem is that which arises when one's individual principles are at variance with those laid down in a conventional society. In Germany " honor " is not so much a personal matter as a fixed code applicable to situations, and an individual who finds himself in a certain situation must have recourse to the code, not his own convictions. Sudermann in this play sets himself the task of opposing the current conception of honor, and in Trast's mouth he places what arguments he wishes to have advanced. Trast is what the French call the " raisonneur ": he who reasons. This method is a very direct but rather bald one, as the audience is likely, nowadays at least, to resent a preacher who is only too obviously doing his duty. It prefers the method followed by another very skilful writer of thesis plays, Brieux, who in his " Red Robe " allows the thesis to unfold itself before the eyes of the spectators rather than permit a raisonneur " to expound his personal ideas. But in Sudermann's day the technic of the drama was not so far advanced as it was twelve years later, when the French dramatist was able to employ means to his end which were artistic in the highest degree.

Yet Sudermann always lacked the sincerity and earnestness of Brieux, for he considered the play primarily as a means to tell a story in as effective a manner as possible. Brieux's purpose has always been to expose a state of affairs and argue about it. As a consequence, Sudermann never fell into the error of allowing the thesis to overshadow the play. As a matter of fact, he became with years less and less didactic, and took good care that his later plays should be free of encumbering theses, so that now his desire to please the unthinking public has brought him near to artistic bankruptcy.

Sudermann is clearly a man whose best work is over. " Honor " led dramatists to treat the theater more seriously, it taught them to construct plays with a story, and showed that a thesis play is not necessarily a " conversation "; his attention to detail instilled a desire for greater truthfulness in the delineation of character. " Honor " and its immediate successors present a series of pictures of lower, middle, and upper class German society of the day which are and will in the future prove of great value for the student of the times and of the drama.

BARRETT H. CLARK.

PERSONS REPRESENTED.

COUNCILLOR OF COMMERCE MUHLINGK
AMALIE..............................*His wife*
KURT } ....*Their children*
LEONORE }
LOTHAR BRANDT
HUGO STENGEL
COUNT VON TRAST-SAARBERG
RORERT HEINECKE
OLD HEINECKE
HIS WIFE
AUGUSTE } ....*Their daughters*
ALMA }
MICHALSKI..........*A joiner, Auguste's husband*
FRAU HEBENSTREIT...*The* ⎫
       Gardener's wife ⎬ *In Muhlingk's service*
WILHELM......*A servant* ⎪
JOHANN....... *Coachman* ⎭
INDIAN SERVANT OF COUNT TRAST

The action takes place in the vicinity of Charlottenburg, now a part of Berlin.

HONOR

ACT I.

SCENE:—*A room in* HEINECKE'S *house—The cheap,
lower middle-class decorations and tawdry furnishings are in sharp contrast with two silk-up-
holstered arm-chairs, which are covered during
the first part of the act—and a large gilded mirror. A chest of drawers and several shelves
are covered with various worn articles of
household use. To the right of the spectator,
below the traditional German sofa, is a table
with a coffee service. To the left is a long,
rough-hewn work-table; upon it are pieces of
cardboard, a pile of cardboard boxes and a
large paste-pot. Beside the table is a work-
stool.*

(FRAU HEINECKE *is busily engaged in cleaning the
room.* FRAU HEBENSTREIT *stands on the
threshold of the door to the left.*)

FRAU HEBENSTREIT.   So it's really true?—Your
son is home?

FRAU HEINECKE.   Sh! sh!—for the Lord's sake
—he's asleep!

FRAU HEBENSTREIT.   There is Alma's bedroom?

FRAU HEINECKE.   Yes!—I don't know what I'm
about!—I'm actually dizzy from joy! (*Drops into
the work-stool*)

9

FRAU HEBENSTREIT.   Do the folks on the avenue
know about it yet? *

FRAU HEINECKE.   He had to report to 'em to-day
because they're his boss.   To-morrow he'll make the
visit.

FRAU HEBENSTREIT.   How long has he been gone,
anyway?

FRAU HEINECKE.   Seven—eight—nine and a half
years.   It's as long as that since I've seen my boy!
(*She sobs*)

FRAU HEBENSTREIT.   And did you recognize him
right off?

FRAU HEINECKE.   Well, how should I?   Last
night about eight—Heinecke was half asleep over
the Lokal Anzeiger,† and I'm sitting there sewing
a lace hem on Alma's underwaist,—that girl's always got to have something new for her underwear!
—Well, all of a sudden there was a knock, and a
man come in, and Lord save us if there didn't stand
a gentleman, a fine gentleman in a beaver coat—
there it hangs!—just feel that beaverskin once!—I
thought to myself: it's one of Alma's swell ac-
quaintances, one of young Herr Kurt's friends——

FRAU   HEBENSTREIT.   (*Listening   attentively*)
Ah——

FRAU HEINECKE.   For they ain't too stuck up to
come around and see us poor folks on the alley—
Well, as I was saying, he throws his hat and coat on
the floor—a real top hat—right down on the floor,
mind you!—and he gets right down on his knees in
front of me—well, I thought I was losing my mind,
but when he calls out: " Mother, Father, don't you
know me?—It's me, Robert, your son Robert "--

*Certain German houses are divided into two parts the
so-called " Hinterhaus " and " Vorderhaus."   The " Vorderhaus " (translated roughly " on the avenue ") is the
larger part and usually belongs to the owner.   The
" Hinterhaus " (rendered " on the alley ") is a few rooms
opening on an alleyway or court whose occupants sometimes act in the capacity of caretakers, but who often
have nothing to do with the people in the Vorderhaus
and hardly consider themselves on a plane with the
richer family's servants.—Tr.

†A newspaper.—Tr.

Well, Frau Hebenstreit, it was just too good to be true! I'll never get over it! (*She cries*)

FRAU HEBENSTREIT. Don't get excited, neighbor; the pleasure won't last! Every rat has a head and tail—and a rat's tail is poison, they do say.

FRAU HEINECKE. How can you say a thing like that! My son is a good son, a fine son.

FRAU HEBENSTREIT. Too fine, Frau Heinecke! When a person's been traveling around in all them foreign lands and living in silks and satins——

FRAU HEINECKE. He can have all that here—(*Indicating the silk upholstered chairs*)

FRAU HEBENSTREIT. (*With a grimace*) Yes, yes,—but whether he will or not——

FRAU HEINECKE. Whether he will or not, Frau Hebenstreit! A mother's heart don't reckon with rank and society!—And—Good Lord! Here I am a-standing—Where on earth can Heinecke be? Have you seen Heinecke?—The way he has to hobble along with his lame leg!

FRAU HEBENSTREIT. I saw him standing outside with a sign as big as all outdoors, drying his sign he said—and the thermometer at thirty above zero!

FRAU HEINECKE. Let the old man enjoy himself. He was working on that sign half the night. Couldn't sleep a wink—neither of us—we was so happy——

(HEINECKE *enters, limping, with a huge placard. One of his arms is stiff.*)

HEINECKE. Hurrah! Now we've——

FRAU HEINECKE. Will you be still!

HEINECKE. (*Reading the placard*) " Welcome, beloved son, to your father's house." Fine, eh?

FRAU HEBENSTREIT. Looks for all the world like a target!

HEINECKE. With a heart in the middle! You old—!

Frau Heinecke. Hold your tongue!—(*To* Frau Hebenstreit) You know how he is!

(Heinecke *takes a hammer and tacks and climbs on chair to tack up the placard.*)

Frau Hebenstreit. I wonder where your son got all his fine manners anyway? Not from *his* family, did he?

Frau Heinecke. No, nor mine either. It was seventeen years ago, when our boss on the avenue got his title of Councillor of Commerce—there was a great time: carriages and fireworkings and free beer for all the workmen in the factory. Well, my husband was a little bit full—and why not?— Pa, quit pounding! when it didn't cost nothing? Well, one of the carriages run over him,—broke his leg and his arm!

Heinecke. (*Standing on the stool*) Talking about me? Yes, that wasn't no joke, neither! (*Whistles*)

Frau Heinecke. Don't whistle! The folks in front can hear that from the balcony, and they'll send round to find out what's the matter with our family affairs!—And the boss was so tickled over his new title, that he was feelin' free with his pocket-book and he promised to take care of us and give our oldest an education.

Frau Hebenstreit. And did he stick to it?

Heinecke. (*Working*) Ah, there!

Frau Heinecke. Couldn't 've done better! They gave us a place here on the alley, where, thank God, we still are, and they sent Robert off to the school where he got his learning. And when he came back home on his vacations, he was always invited over on the avenue to drink chocolate with whip-cream,—on purpose to play with the little Miss. Young Herr Kurt was still sucking a rubber nipple then.

FRAU HEBENSTREIT. That was all before Alma—?

FRAU HEINECKE. (*More quietly*) What do you mean by that?

FRAU HEBENSTREIT. Aw, nothing, I——

FRAU HEINECKE. And then afterwards they sent him to Hamburg to learn about the foreign business, you know—and when he was seventeen off he goes to India, where they say it's so outlandish hot! The Councillor's nephew is out there. He's got a big coffee and tea plantation!

HEINECKE. It grows out there just like daisies do around here! (*Gets down from the stool*) Fine, eh?

FRAU HEINECKE. And he got along pretty well out there, and, Lord, here he is home again and I stand around and——

FRAU HEBENSTREIT. I'm a-going. Good-bye, and don't forget the poison in the rat's tail! (*Aside*) It's a pretty kettle of fish! (*She goes out*)

HEINECKE. She's an old poison-toad herself!

FRAU HEINECKE. Jealousy—jealousy—jealousy!

HEINECKE. Well! Where did you get the pound-cake!

FRAU HEINECKE. The cook brought it, with the compliments of the Miss,

HEINECKE. (*Turning away*) What comes from the avenue don't interest me! The boy must have had enough sleep by this time. The factory whistle will blow for the second lunch * in a minute! (*Looking lovingly at the placard*) " Welcome, beloved son——"

FRAU HEINECKE. (*Suddenly*) Father, he's here!

HEINECKE. Who?

FRAU HEINECKE. Our boy!

*The German workman is allowed time in the middle of the morning for a light lunch which tides him over from his coffee and rolls to the more substantial dinner at noon.—Tr.

HEINECKE. (*Pointing to placard*) We're ready for him!

FRAU HEINECKE. Shh! I heard something! (*Listening*) Yes, I told you! He's putting on his shoes. When I think of it! There he is a-sitting putting on his shoes, and in a minute he'll come through this door——

HEINECKE. All I'll say is: "Welcome, beloved "·—did you put some of that swell soap of Alma's on his washstand?

FRAU HEINECKE. And how many times have I set here and thought to myself: has he even got a decent bed under him?—and—and—have the savages eaten him up already? And now all of a sudden here he is, Father—Father we've got him again! May the luck keep up!

HEINECKE. Look here a minute—does this look all right?

FRAU HEINECKE. Quiet!—He's coming. Your tie's slipped up again! I'm ashamed of you! (*Smoothes the cover of the arm-chair*) Lord, how nervous I am!

(ROBERT *bursts into the room and runs to his parents, who stand stiffly before him, embarrassed.*)

ROBERT. Good morning, Father!—Good morning, Mother! (*He embraces his mother and repeatedly kisses her hand*) I am—absolutely—inhumanly—happy!

HEINECKE. "Welcome, beloved son "—(*As* ROBERT *bows over his hand he rubs it on his trousers*) You're going to kiss my hand?!!

ROBERT. Certainly, if you'll let me!

HEINECKE. (*Extending his hand*) Now you can see what a good son he is!

ROBERT. (*Looking about*) And here is where I once—I hardly know—is it really possible?—Or am I actually dreaming still? That would be too bad—Oh,—and the homesickness!—Lord in heaven, that homesickness!—Just think! You sit out there at night in some corner, and everything you have left appears about you, living;—mother, father,—the court, the garden, the factory—and then all of a sudden you see the long palm branches waving over you, or a parrot screams in the distance and you come to yourself and realise that you are all alone at the other end of the world! Brrr!

HEINECKE. Parrots? That must be nice! Here only the rich folks can have 'em!

ROBERT. Yes, and if you only knew how I worried these last years, and even on the journey home, for fear I shouldn't find everything the way my longing had painted it!

HEINECKE. Why?

RORERT. There was a man—otherwise a dear friend, my best friend, too—who tried to prepare me for disappointment. You have become foreign, he said, and you shouldn't try to put together what Fate has separated so long ago—Heaven knows what else he said—and I was almost afraid of him, and you, and myself too! Thank God that doesn't bother me any more; every single thing has come out as I hoped! Everything I had imagined for ten years is exactly as I expected—there is Father— there's Mother, sweet and simple and (*Tenderly*) a bit of a chatterbox! (*Stretching himself*) But what are these two young arms for? Just watch! They've learned to make money!—And the sisters will soon be ready too! Just see!—And here is father's old paste-pot—(*Strokes the paste-pot*) And my confirmation certificate—framed! And the machinery makes the same, dear old noise!

FRAU HEINECKE. You never slept a wink on account of that old machine—eh? It bumps and bangs the whole night!

ROBERT. I was never sung to sleep by a sweeter lullaby, Mother. When I was almost asleep I kept saying: snort if you want, puff if you like, you old horse! Keep at it, but work as you will while I am lying here in bed, *you* can't do anything for the glory of the house of Muhlingk. *Here* is a lever that must be reckoned with! Wasn't that a proud thought?—And then my heart warmed for our benefactor.

HEINECKE. Huh!

RORERT. What, Father?

HEINECKE. Aw, nuthin'!

ROBERT. And I have sworn that I won't slacken in his service until I've drawn my last breath!

HEINECKE. I should think by this time you'd have done about enough for them!

FRAU HEINECKE. You've scraped and slaved for them for ten years!

ROBERT. Oh, it wasn't as bad as that, Mother. But now let's not talk about them this way any more. Every day we have one reason or other for thanking the Muhlingks. The letters I had from the Councillor, and from Kurt especially,—he's a partner now,—were like letters from a close friend.

HEINECKE. Kurt—Oh, he's a fine young gentleman! But as for the rest—" The Moor has paid his debt " * as the Berliner says—show me the rabble! (ROBERT *swallows his answer and turns away, frowning*) But, Bobby, look around! Don't you notice anything? He don't see anything, Mother!

FRAU HEINECKE. Oh, stop your chatter!

HEINECKE. Chatter! Ho! When I try to welcome my dear son back to his father's house, then it's chatter! (*Leads* ROBERT *to the placard*) W—what do you say to that, eh?

ROBERT. Did you make that, Father, you with your lame arm?

HEINECKE. Ah! I make lots of things. If the poor old cripple didn't take a hand this fine family would have starved long ago!—(*Rather roughly*)

*A well known quotation from Schiller's " Die Rauber. "

What are you standing there staring at, Mother? Where's the coffee?

FRAU HEINECKE. Well, well! (*Starts to go*)

ROBERT. (*Hurrying after her*) Oh, Mother, he didn't mean anything!

FRAU HEINECKE. Mean anything? Ha! Ha! he's only talking that way to make you think he's the man of the house! (*She goes out*)

ROBERT. (*After a pause, he tries to smoothe over the unpleasantness*) You still paste boxes, Father?

HEINECKE. Still at it!

ROBERT. And the arm doesn't bother you?

HEINECKE. My arm, ha! ha! ha! my arm! Do you want to see how I do it! First the pasteboard—so—then the fold—so! (*With great speed he sweeps the pastebrush across two sheets of cardboard, pressing them into place with his left elbow*) Who could beat your old cripple at that?

ROBERT. You are a regular juggler.

HEINECKE. That's what! But who admits it? Who appreciates me? Who appreciates me? Nobody! How could the daughters—one of 'em already a Missus—respect me when their own mother gives 'em such a bad example!

ROBERT. (*Indignantly*) Father!

HEINECKE. Yes, you're a long way from her lap—far away cows have long horns—There, it's " dear little Mother! sweet little sister! "—But if you knew what I've had to stand! Not once does she give me horse-car-fare when I want to go to town for a glass of beer!

ROBERT. Are you quite fair to her? Doesn't she cherish you as the apple of her eye?

HEINECKE. Lord, I didn't mean to say anything against her—shh!—here she comes! (*Enter* FRAU HEINECKE *with a steaming coffee-pot*) Sit down, Bobby,—No, here in the arm-chair! Wait a minute! (*Pulls off the covering from the chair*) Such a fine gentleman ought to sit on pure silk!

ROBERT.   Heavens, what luxury!

FRAU HEINECKE.   Yes, and the other's just the same!   Two pieces we've got!   And have you seen the pier-glass?   All gold creepers, and the glass in one piece!   Augusta's husband says it cost at least two hundred marks!

ROBERT.   Where did all these wonderful things come from.

FRAU HEINECKE.   From the Councillor!

ROBERT.   He gives you things like this?

HEINECKE.   Naw, only——

FRAU HEINECKE.   (*Aside*)   Ssh! don't you know that Herr Kurt doesn't want it known?   (*To* ROBERT)   Yes, last Christmas he gave us the mirror, and this Christmas the two chairs.   Father, quit boring holes in the pound cake!

ROBERT.   Really, I don't like this sort of generosity!

FRAU HEINECKE.   (*Pouring out coffee*)   This furniture 'd be too good for some people!   But when we have such fine visitors and such a distinguished gentleman for a son, and such an awful talented daughter——

ROBERT.   Alma?

HEINECKE.   Yessir!   We did everything for our girl we were able to do.

FRAU HEINECKE.   And   you   always   sent money——

ROBERT.   So that she should have a proper schooling, and learn millinery and bookkeeping. That's what we agreed on.

FRAU HEINECKE.   Yes—that was before—!

ROBERT.   Before?   Hasn't she the same position now?

FRAU HEINECKE.   Not for the last six months.

ROBERT.   What is she doing now?

HEINECKE.   (*Proudly*)   She is cultivating her voice!

ROBERT.   Why, I never heard she was musical!

HEINECKE. Awful musical!

(*They drink the coffee.*)

FRAU HEINECKE. She was examined by some
Italian singer—Seenyora or something—she said
she had never heard anything like it before and she
would take it as an honor to develop Alma's voice
herself at her own cost.

ROBERT. But why did you keep that from me?

FRAU HEINECKE. Oh, it was such a long way,
clear out to India, you forget such things—and
then, we wanted to give you a surprise!

ROBERT. (*Gets up and walks excitedly up and
down*) Auguste really takes good care of her?

FRAU HEINECKE. Certainly. She never lets her
eye off her. Alma eats at her house and practises
at her house and when she stays too late to catch the
horsecar she sleeps there—same as she did last
night.

ROBERT. And when she stays away all night,
doesn't that worry you?

HEINECKE. Huh! Big girl like that!

FRAU HEINECKE. No, not when we've brought
her up so well—and she's with Auguste, too! She
ought to be here soon. The milk-man took the let-
ter over early. How surprised she'll be!

ROBERT. And Auguste is happy?

FRAU HEINECKE. Oh, so—so. Her husband
boozes a little, and when it comes to working, he
ain't much, but——

HEINECKE. But when it comes to sulking and
raising Cain, he's right at home!

FRAU HEINECKE. But, all in all, they get along
all right. Auguste has furnished up two swell
rooms, and rented 'em to a gentleman from Pots-
dam that ain't there half the time, but pays for the
whole month! That brings in many a pretty penny.
He pays a whole mark just for his coffee in the
morning. (*Goes to the window*) There she comes!
And she's brought her husband along, too!

ROBERT. What? Isn't Alma with her?

(AUGUSTE *and* MICHALSKI *come in.*)

AUGUSTE. Well, well, here you are! (*They kiss each other*) Everything has been going fine with you, hasn't it? What's the use of asking? When a man goes around in clothes like those!—Of course everything ain't gold that glitters—here's my husband!

ROBERT. Well, brother-in-law, give me your hand,—one of the family!

MICHALSKI. Honored! Don't often happen that a horny hand like this is so honored!

ROBERT. That doesn't sound very brotherly. (*To* AUGUSTE) Where's Alma?

AUGUSTE. Our Princess was afraid she wasn't beautiful enough for the foreign brother! She had to stay and burn her bangs first. (ROBERT *is deeply concerned*) She'll probably come by the next car. Where did you get the pound-cake? (FRAU HEINECKE *passes the cake around and* MICHALSKI *and* AUGUSTE *eat*)

FRAU HEINECKE. Eat another piece, Bobby!

(ROBERT *refuses, but the others eat.*)

HEINECKE. (*After a pause*) What do you say to that, Michalski, " Welcome, beloved son."

MICHALSKI. (*Eating*) Nonsense!

ROBERT. (*Surprised*) Brother-in-law!

HEINECKE. What? What I did with this noble heart and this lame arm!

(ROBERT *pacifies him.*)

MICHALSKI. I'm a simple man and I ain't afraid to say what I think! I've got no use for that kind of rot and nonsense! When a man has got to work the way we do with his stomach empty and a whip at his back——

HEINECKE. 'Specially when a man goes walking at eleven o'clock and eats pound-cake to boot!

AUGUSTE. Are you two at it again? (*To* MICHALSKI) Will you never shut up? Can't you see he's in his second childhood?

HEINECKE. I'm in—Good!—Now you see! That's the way I'm treated by my own children!

ROBERT. (*Aside to* AUGUSTE) Really, sister, I never thought you would say a thing like that!

AUGUSTE. What are you talking about?

(*Enter* WILHELM.)

ALL. (*Except* ROBERT) It's Wilhelm! Good morning, Wilhelm! (HEINECKE *and* MICHALSKI *shake hands with him*)

FRAU HEINECKE. Who is the pretty bouquet for? That must be for somebody in the city.

WILHELM. No, it's for you . . . You are the young gentleman? (ROBERT *nods—cordially*) Awful glad to know you! (*About to offer his hand*)

ROBERT. (*Smiling*) Very kind of you.

WILHELM. The honorable family sends you a hearty welcome and these flowers. They are the rarest in the conservatory. But, between you and me, the flowers came from the Gnadiges Fraulein. And the Gnadiges Fraulein was pretty anxious to——

ROBERT. Were you commissioned to say that, too? (*Controlling his feelings*)

WILHELM. No, not——

ROBERT. Then keep it to yourself!

(*The servant starts to go.*)

FRAU HEINECKE. Wouldn't you like to have a piece of pound-cake with us, Wilhelm? There's plenty left!

ROBERT. Please, Mother! (*Gives* WILHELM *a gold-piece*) The man has his pay—Tell the Councillor that the Count von Trast-Saarburg and I **beg** the honor of a meeting with him at three o'clock! You may go! (WILHELM *goes*)

FRAU HEINECKE. A count! What sort of a count?

ROBERT. A friend of mine, Mother, to whom I am under great obligation.

AUGUSTE. (*Softly to* MICHALSKI) He pretends to have a count for a friend!

FRAU HEINECKE. Wait, I'll put the flowers in water. But you oughtn't to have been so harsh with Wilhelm, Bobby! He's a good friend of ours.

AUGUSTE. Us common folks don't have counts for friends!

MICHALSKI. We have to be contented with servants!

FRAU HEINECKE. Yes, you must be nice to Wilhelm, Robert, for our sakes; he can do a lot for us! How many pieces of roasts and how many bottles of wine has he slipped us!

ROBERT. And you accepted them, Mother?

FRAU HEINECKE. Why not, my boy! We're poor folks—we ought to be glad to get things like that for nothing!

ROBERT. Mother, I'll double my efforts; I'll give you what I can spare for my bare living expenses. But promise me you won't take anything more from that servant, will you?

FRAU HEINECKE. Oh, that would be foolish pride and waste! You should not look a gift-horse in the mouth! And he only wanted to do you a favor, when he told you that about the Gnadiges Fraulein! That's something special! Whenever I met her in the court, there wasn't a single time when she didn't stop me and ask if there was any news from you, and how you got on with the hot weather and all! And at the same time she smiled so friendly—if you were a smart boy, Robert——

ROBERT. For heaven's sake, Mother, stop!

HEINECKE. That wouldn't be so bad—two millions!

MICHALSKI. Would you lend me a little then, eh, Brother-in-law?

ROBERT. (*To himself*) How much longer must I be tortured?

(ALMA *appears at the half-open door. She wears a yellow jacket and a coquettish little hat. She wears suede gloves and many bracelets. She carries a fancy parasol.*)

ALMA. Good morning, everybody.

ROBERT. (*Runs to her and embraces her*) Alma! Thank God!

MICHALSKI. (*To* AUGUSTE) The two swells of the family!

AUGUSTE. (*Lovingly*) Listen: little sister, if you were as ugly as you are pretty, you wouldn't take long to find out that your brother hated you.

ALMA. Auguste, that's mean.

ROBERT. Oh, she didn't mean anything. Now be good again!

ALMA. (*Affected*) My own dear brother!

AUGUSTE. (*Aside*) Lord, ain't it touching!

(FRAU HEINECKE *helps* ALMA *off with her jacket.*)

HEINECKE. Now what do you say? (*Stroking her cheek*) Are you my little treasure or not, eh?

ALMA. (*Trilling*) "Oui, cher papa! c'est Girofla!"

HEINECKE. Do you hear how she sings? Real Italian!

ROBERT. Now what's this I hear: you want to be a great singer?

ALMA. Well, I'd not object to that!

FRAU HEINECKE. Won't you eat a little piece of pound-cake, Alma?

ALMA. Merci beaucoup! (*Goes about in front of the mirror, eating*)

ROBERT. And you are studying hard?

ALMA. (*Her mouth full of cake*) I have lessons every afternoon—Do, re, mi, fa, sol, la, si—si, la sol.—fa—Oh, those scales! Terrible bore! And practice—Eternal practice!—My nerves are ruined already!

FRAU HEINECKE. Poor child!

ALMA. "Oh, yes, Ma!"* I've been studying English, too! I'm awfully cultured.—Oh, what I've learned!

HEINECKE. Yes sir! D'ye see!

ALMA. And above all—we only live once—have a good time, that's the main thing! Are you happy, too, brother?

ROBERT. Certainly, when I have reason to be.

ALMA. The great art is to be happy without any reason. Why are we young? Oh, it's good to live! Every day something new!—And Berlin is so lovely! You know—the Linden!—and the electric light! Have you seen it yet? That's what I like the best of all. Everybody is so pretty and pale, so interesting!—And the restaurants have all got electric lights now, too. Grand!—I saw a chandelier in a cafe in the Donhoffplatz—it was a great big wreath of flowers and every flower had a light in it!

ROBERT. Were you in the cafe?

ALMA. I? How could I be? Through the window it was! You don't have things like that in India? Do you?

ROBERT. No, we certainly don't.

ALMA. We're pretty far advanced in culture here. Somebody told me that Berlin was almost as beautiful as Paris. Is that so?

ROBERT. I don't know Paris, dear.

ALMA. Ugh! That's a shame! Every young man ought to know Paris.

*Thus in the original.—Tr.

ROBERT. (*Charmed, yet shocked by her vulgarity*) You little silly!

ALMA. Ha! ha! ha! I'm a funny one! don't you think? Ha! ha! Yes, that's the way! (*She goes about laughing, and rocks back and forth. She takes a little handkerchief, which she carries folded in triangular form in her belt; and holds it under* AUGUSTE'S *nose*) Smell it?

AUGUSTE. (*Aside*) Fine! What's that?

ALMA. (*Aside*) Ixora, the very latest from Paris—got it to-day!

AUGUSTE. Coming out to-night?

ALMA. Don't know! He'll send me word—But to-morrow evening we're going to the masked ball! Ha! ha!

ROBERT. Now let's be sensible again, little one. Come here—Sit down—Here! Here!

ALMA. Heavens! How you act! This is going to be a regular cross-examination!

ROBERT. I'm going to ask you a lot of questions.

(FRAU *and* HERR HEINECKE *group themselves about* ALMA'S *chair.* MICHALSKI *sits on the work table,* AUGUSTE *beside him on the stool.*)

ALMA. Go ahead! S'il vous plait, Monsieur!

MICHALSKI. (*Aside to* AUGUSTE) This will be a nice mess!

ROBERT. How did you happen to discover this talent?

ALMA. It comes like love—can't tell how!

ROBERT. (*Unpleasantly affected*) Hum—But someone must have told you about it!

(ALMA *shrugs her shoulders.*)

FRAU HEINECKE. Don't you remember, child? It was Herr Kurt that——

ROBERT. The young manager?

HEINECKE. Certainly.

ROBERT. But how did he know——?

FRAU HEINECKE. He heard her singing—through the window on the court. And the next thing, he said it was a sin and a shame that a voice like hers——

ROBERT. But why do you let Mother tell everything, Alma?

AUGUSTE. (*To* MICHALSKI) She's so modest.

ALMA. That a voice like mine should be wasted here in the alley—and that *I* should not be wasted here in the alley, for that matter! It's really an imposition on you, Gnadiges Fraulein, he said!

FRAU HEINECKE. I heard that myself: " Gnadiges Fraulein! "

HEINECKE. My daughter, yes sir!

ROBERT. Go ahead, Alma!

ALMA. My parents took care of your brother, he said,—I'll take care of you!—Well, and then he found a teacher for me who held a *cercle musical*—that means a musical circle—made up of young ladies of the best families.—One is engaged to a lieutenant of the Hussars.

ROBERT. And what is the teacher's name?

ALMA. (*Suspicously*) What do you want to know for?

ROBERT. Because it can't be any secret!

ALMA. Her name is Signora Paulucci.

HEINECKE. (*Enthusiastically*) Real Italian!

ROBERT. (*Taking out his note-book*) And her address?

ALMA. (*Quickly*) You don't need to go there. It's true!

ROBERT. Of course it's true. But I'd like to hear the teacher's own opinion about your voice. (ALMA *looks quickly toward* AUGUSTE)

AUGUSTE. You can go to her lesson with her to-morrow.

ALMA. Yes, to-morrow!

ROBERT. Good! (*Gets up and walks back and forth excitedly*) I don't want to make you feel badly, dear, but I must admit I don't share your great hopes.

HEINECKE. Eh?

ROBERT. How many a young girl is enticed into these things purely through ambition and vanity! And it's dangerous! More dangerous than you realize—Of course I am sure that the young manager has the highest and the noblest of motives, but —Well, however that may be, to-morrow I'll hear myself what the teacher says, and if my doubts are groundless, I promise to take care of you myself, and we shan't rest a moment until you have reached the climax of your art! (ALMA *takes the vase from the table and buries her face in the flowers*) Wouldn't it be strange if we were to owe everything —even this piece of good fortune—to the house of Muhlingk!

(MICHALSKI *laughs mockingly.*)

ALMA. Mama, who sent me this bouquet?

FRAU HEINECKE. That's a welcome to—(*Indicates* ROBERT) from the Gnadiges Fraulein!

ALMA. Oh, from her! (*She puts down the vase*)

ROBERT. Wait a minute! One question! It seems that every time I mention the " Avenue " or any of the family, someone bursts out laughing, or makes some disapproving remark. Herr Muhlingk junior is the only one who seems to meet with your approval. Now, frankly, what have you against *our* benefactor? What has he done to offend you? (*A pause*) You, for instance, Brother-in-law, what made you laugh so scornfully? (*Silence*) Or you, Alma, that you won't have anything to do with the flowers that came from Miss Muhlingk! Mother just told me how kind she has always been!

ALMA. Kind, is she? She's a stuck-up thing,

that can't poke her nose high enough in the air when she meets me!—Never says a word to me; why, it's all she can do to return my bow! Oh, she——!

AUGUSTE. She's the same way to me.

ROBERT. (*Sorrowfully, to himself*) That isn't like her!

FRAU HEINECKE. (*Tenderly*) Just wait till she marries my boy!

ROBERT. (*Shocked,—interrupting her*) Mother! But I'd forgotten: I've brought some presents for my sisters, and you, too, Brother-in-law.

AUGUSTE. (*Jumping up greedily*) What have you got? Where is it?

ROBERT. In the bed-room. There's a card with each one's name on it.

(*The three, AUGUSTE ahead, hurry into the bedroom.*)

HEINECKE. And you've got nothing for us?

ROBERT. There wasn't anything out there good enough for you, dear parents. Tell me what you want?

FRAU HEINECKE. If I should see the day when I had a sofa to match them arm-chairs—(*She sees that ROBERT is staring ahead without listening to her*) But you ain't listening!

ROBERT. (*Sadly reproving*) No, mother, I wasn't listening!

HEINECKE. (*Defiantly*) And I want a new paste-pot—you ought to be able to afford that! (*The three come back from the bedroom. AUGUSTE carries a colored shawl, ALMA a jewel-case, MICHALSKI a Turkish pipe. They surround ROBERT and thank him*)

AUGUSTE. What a pity they don't wear Indian shawls any more!

MICHALSKI. (*Puffing at the stem of his pipe*) Course it don't draw!

ROBERT. (*To* ALMA, *who is playing with her jewels*) Are you satisfied, Alma? Look at the three blue stones, they are Indian sapphire.

ALMA. Very pretty! But to tell the truth, I like the dark-blue sapphires more! They have such beautiful brilliancy!

ROBERT. How do you know so much about such things?

ALMA. Oh—from the shop windows! People of our sort like to look in windows!

ROBERT. And what's that shining in your ear?

ALMA. Paste, that's all! Two Marks a pair!

ROBERT. Dear, you mustn't wear things like that!—Promise me you'll take them off this minute —and I'll show you another special surprise that I've brought you.

ALMA. (*Sullenly, taking off the ear-rings*) As you please!

ROBERT. It's the dress of a hindoo Princess— looted on a military invasion undertaken by a friend of mine. Think of it! Pink and gold!

ALMA. (*Joyfully*) Oh, how heavenly!

MICHALSKI. (*Laughing*) And I s'pose you hung her up stark naked on a tree!

(ROBERT *stares at him.*)

ALMA. (*Lovingly*) You're a dear, sweet, old brother!

(*A coachman in livery knocks at the window.*)

FRAU HEINECKE. Go, see what Johann wants, Father.

ALMA. (*To* AUGUSTE) Oh, but they'll all turn green with envy when I wear this to the masked ball to-morrow.

AUGUSTE. Shh!

HEINECKE. (*From the window*) Johann says

Herr Kurt is going to drive to the city at three, and he wants to know if you'd like to go along.

(*Alma and* AUGUSTE *exchange glances.*)

ROBERT. What does that mean?

AUGUSTE. Simple enough! Herr Kurt has his carriage, and since he's an obliging young man he gave Alma a standing invitation to ride to the city with him.

ROBERT. What? She allowed that? You, sister, you accepted that?

ALMA. A poor girl ought to be glad enough to ride in a carriage once in a while!

FRAU HEINECKE. And you save car-fare!

ROBERT. Good heavens! And what do the ladies on the Avenue say to that?

ALMA. Oh, they don't know anything about it! When I ride with him he stops the carriage at the back doorway where only the tradespeople go in.

ROBERT. So much the worse! What a disgusting implication in all this secrecy! Alma, haven't you felt that yourself?—Alma, come here!—Look me in the eyes.

ALMA. (*Staring at him*) Well?

ROBERT. (*Takes her head in both his*) You are pure!—you are—(*He kisses her cheeks and forehead*)

HEINECKE. Decide, now! Johann is waiting!

ROBERT. Tell Johann, Father, that I'll speak to his master about it first.

ALMA. What for? It's all been arranged already.

ROBERT. You won't use Herr Muhlingk's carriage any more! For a girl of your—our position, there is always the street-car!

(ALMA *begins to cry defiantly.*)

FRAU HEINECKE. The poor child!

AUGUSTE. You seem to want to turn everything in this house upside down!

(*Children's voices are heard in the court.*)

HEINECKE. Come here!—Quick!—A Moor!—in a turban!

ALL. (*Except* ROBERT, *who remains, troubled, rush to the window*) That's not a Moor!

ALMA. (*Still sobbing*) Robert—is that—a Moor?

ROBERT. (*Darkly*) No, that's my friend's Indian servant.

FRAU HEINECKE. Your friend?—is that the count?

ROBERT. Yes.

(*The servant comes in, and they crowd about him.*)

ROBERT. Ragharita, your master is welcome in the house of my father!

(*Servant goes out. Great excitement.* FRAU HEINECKE *draws out the arm-chairs and polishes the mirror.*)

ALMA. (*From the mirror*) Is your count young or old? (ROBERT *makes no answer*) My eyes are red!—Red as fire, aren't they, Auguste? And he may be young! (*She goes out, left*)

MICHALSKI. Come, Auguste, we won't disturb the great gentlemen!

HEINECKE. Herr Count, I'll say, take a seat in this arm-chair, I'll say! Oh, we know how to act with the nobility!

FRAU HEINECKE. There was a baron here once —a gentleman friend of Herr Kurt. Don't you remember, Father? He came to ask after Alma— But a count! we never had a count!

ROBERT. Who did you say had been here, Mother?

(*Enter* COUNT TRAST, *a man between forty and*

*fifty, with gray hair and a long, blond beard.
He is dressed with careless foreign elegance.
ROBERT rushes to him and takes his hand.*)

TRAST. (*Aside to* ROBERT) How is this? Hasn't
the home fever abated yet! (*Aloud*) So here we
have the long-expected son! (*Shakes his hand*)
Do you know, my fine people, that a sort of foster-
son of yours is standing here? The friendship with
this dear old comrade of mine gives me almost a
right to that title!

(HEINECKE *tiptoes out of the door.*)

FRAU HEINECKE. Wouldn't the Count like a
piece of pound-cake? There is still some there.
TRAST. Thanks, I shall be glad—I certainly
shall!

(FRAU HEINECKE *curtseys out of the room.*)

TRAST. You're pale, my boy, and your hands are
shaking—what's wrong?
ROBERT. Oh, nothing! The happiness—the ex-
citement! It's only natural!
TRAST. Naturally! (*Aside*) He's lying! (*To*
ROBERT) Tell me, how long do you intend to stay
here? I want to regulate my stay in this great
Europe by that!
ROBERT. That's impossible, my friend! Our
ways will have to part!
TRAST. Nonsense!
ROBERT. I shall ask my employer to give me a
position here. The climate in India—you under-
stand——?
TRAST. That's pleasant! He doesn't want to
leave his mother's apron-strings again, eh?
ROBERT. Don't make fun of me. Since we're
going to part—I have to say it some time—I thank

you, you kind old wicked fellow, for all you've done for me. It was the most fortunate moment of my life when you saw me standing feverishly behind my young employer in the Club at Buitenzorg, when he was throwing one hundred-gulden note after the other onto the green cloth.

TRAST. Why was I such a fool? If you're going to—Ugh! It isn't decent!

ROBERT. Trast! don't hurt me. See, I owe everything to you. When I heard your name then —the name of Trast and Company that is known from Yokohama to Aden, I felt as though I were standing before the Kaiser himself!

TRAST. Kaiser, by the grace of coffee!

ROBERT. Muhlingk's undertaking in Batavia was on the road to ruin that minute.

TRAST. No wonder, when it had the worst good-for-nothing in the Archipelago for its head.

ROBERT. There was nothing ahead of me but failure and discharge. And then you took the poor home-sick clerk under your pinion, your name opened a hundred doors for me and I grew up into manhood under your care! And Herr Benno Muhlingk led his merry life as he pleased, and I ran the entire business.

TRAST. And the end of the story is that the firm of Muhlingk, along with its clever representative, is a few thousands richer because of us. It's a shame! you ought to have profited by it yourself. Well, I'll open your employer's eyes to the kind of a man you've been! If he doesn't at least make you a partner, I shall declare such a corner in coffee, in my righteous wrath, that the noble German oak-leaf * shall be valued as never before. But, seriously, why do you insist on this caprice of remaining with the Muhlingks? I offer you a tremendous salary and a pair of trousers every Christmas.

*The poor people in Germany drink an infusion of oak-leaves in place of coffee.

(ROBERT *shakes his head*) It isn't only gratitude
that makes a man cling to such an insane idea! Of
course if the inventory of the firm included a fair
German maiden—(*Aside*) Aha! (*To* ROBERT)
Speaking of maidens, just listen to what happened
to me last night. After we had left each other I
wandered aimlessly along the street. A friendly
poster invited into a masked ball. A hundred Indian dancers were to present their exciting dance
according to the advertisement—well, that is my
specialty—I went in. Everything seemed arranged
to lead a young monk to forget his oath. And then
suddenly there came before me a young girl, tender
and fresh as a half-ripe peach. She seemed to be
without a partner. I presented myself. Not at all
bashful, she begged for a little plaything that hung
on my watch-chain, in a little baby voice. It was
my patron saint Ganesa, god of success, who rides
on a little rat. And I smelled a rat myself. What
do you suppose I found beneath her childish innocence? Naif depravity!

ROBERT. (*Nervously*) Are such things possible?

TRAST. Listen. My heart always beats according
to the tempo required by the custom of the land
whose hospitality I am enjoying. I always keep a
harem in the Orient; in Italy I climb the garden
wall by moonlight, in France I pay the dressmaker's
bills, and—Lord!—in Germany—well, I know the
return journey from virtue, too! All according to
rule! In the Orient one loves with his senses, in
Italy with his imagination, in France with his pock-
etbook, in Germany with his conscience! So I tried
to change this sinning child to a repentant Magda-
len. Before I could get started, however, the cham-
pagne had to be uncorked—then came a gentleman,
half demon and half fool, and claimed the lady as
his own. I respected the ancient law of precedence,
and went to bed the poorer by one good act. But
I would give a good deal to know how it happened

that a sweet little thing like—(ROBERT *covers his face with his hands*) Good Lord!—what is it?—Shh!

(*Enter* FRAU HEINECKE.)

FRAU HEINECKE. Bobby!

ROBERT. Mother!

FRAU HEINECKE. Have you got a corkscrew by you? (*To* TRAST) My daughter would like to offer you a bottle of wine. It's no ordinary wine, either, it's the best there is!

ROBERT. Comes from the Avenue, I suppose?

FRAU HEINECKE. (*Proudly*) It does indeed.

ROBERT. There! (*Throws down his knife on the table*)

FRAU HEINECKE. How you *do* act!

ROBERT. Yes, I forgot!—Forgive me!

(FRAU HEINECKE *goes out.*)

TRAST. Now confess, my boy! Trust in me!

ROBERT. Oh, if I had only never seen my home again!

TRAST. Ha! so that's where the wind blows from.

ROBERT. I am ashamed of the position I was born in. My own people have become nothing to me. My whole being shudders from contact with them. I can't trust my mind, one mad suspicion follows the other! Trast! I almost believe I don't even respect the breast that nursed me!

TRAST. That's simply rot!

ROBERT. If I could only explain what I have suffered! Every serious word strikes me like a blow! And every pleasantry like a slap in the face! It seems as though they could talk of nothing but what hurts me—I thought I was coming back to a home,—instead of that it's a strange world where I dare hardly breathe!—Advise me what to do!

TRAST. Pack your trunk!

ROBERT. That would be a cowardly and heartless retreat! Do they deserve that—My own parents!

TRAST. Listen—drop the pathetic note—The matter is simple enough for us. We've studied caste in its native wilds. The same castes exist here. They aren't established by food-laws, or marriage-rules and religious etiquette; those were simple. The chasm that can't be bridged is the difference of feeling—each caste has its own sense of honor, its own nice distinctions, its own ideas, yes, even its own speech. Unhappy is the man who has fallen out of his own caste and hasn't the courage to cut himself off from it entirely. Just such a declasse are you!—and you know, I was the same thing myself! Just what you are feeling now, I went through years ago. How do you suppose I feit, *chic* young cavalry officer, when I woke one morning to the realization that I had gambled away ninety thousand talers that had to be paid in twenty-four hours. What good did it do me to ride home and throw myself at my father's feet? He would have put his head in pawn to save the honor of our name—but he had already done so! And, since he had nothing else to give me, he gave me at least his curse!

ROBERT. (*Brooding*) How you had the courage to live after that!

TRAST. Do you know what happened then?

ROBERT. (*Absently, tortured by his own thoughts*) I know nothing—nothing—nothing!

TRAST. Then listen to me! Perhaps it may be of use to you. When my comrades said farewell to me they did me the last favor of placing a cocked revolver on my table. I looked at the matter from all sides. I took for granted that, without my honor I could not live. Then, as I pointed the thing to my forehead the thought came to me—this is brutal, this is silly! How different are you to-day from what you were three days ago? Perhaps you de-

served punishment for having promised money that
you didn't have; but not death! For thousands of
years men have enjoyed the light of the sun without letting the phantom of honor darken it. To-day
nine hundred and ninety thousands of people belong to that same class, live as they did, and work
as they did, and enjoy the sun as they did! Twelve
years later—of course my debt was long since can-
celled—when I came back to Europe a sort of reconciliation took place between my father and me.
But it was only an outward reconciliation. If he
had found me, like a prodigal son, lying on his door-
step, he would have lifted me up from the dirt with
trembling hands and pressed me to his bosom.
Since I carried my head a little defiantly and was in
a position to help him out with half a million or so
he couldn't forgive me. A few weeks later I left.
The rich coffee seller and the poor cavalier had
nothing in common.

ROBERT. And now he's dead!

TRAST. May he find peace in the heaven he be-
lieved in! Now the moral: leave your parents their
point of view. You can't change that. Give where
there is need—give all you have, and then—come
with me!

ROBERT. I can't! Listen, I'll tell you why. I
didn't tell you before because I was ashamed. I
have a little sister, she was a baby when I left. Oh,
how I longed to see her and looked forward to the
meeting! And I wasn't disappointed, for she was
prettier and sweeter than I had hoped! But my
love for her before a thousand fears I am afraid to
mention! For what she does and lets others do with
her—in perfect innocence, of course—goes against
every feeling of honor I possess! Just now when
you were telling about that girl in the dance-hall; a
cold shiver went through me! Because—no, no, a
thousand times no! Here is my place! I must stay
here, to stand or fall!

TRAST. I admit you have reasons that are at least worth considering. But you are excited. I'll wager you are looking at the dark side!

ROBERT. Would to God! (*He sits down*)

(*Enter* ALMA, *with a tea-tray, upon which is a bottle of wine and three glasses. The Count makes a start,* ALMA *cries out. The tea-tray almost falls*)

TRAST. (*Quickly seizing the situation, steps to her aid*) Came near being a catastrophe, Fraulein! (*Aside*) It is a catastrophe!

ROBERT. See, Trast, this is she! Isn't she an angel? There, give him your hand, and tell him he's welcome!

ALMA. (*Aside*) Don't tell on me—eh?

TRAST. (*Aside*) Poor devil! How can I get him out of it?

CURTAIN.

ACT II.

SCENE:—*The drawing-room in the* MUHLINGK'S *house (The " Vorderhaus"). The furnishings are rich but rather stiff. At the back, a wide door hung with portieres opens into the dining-room. On the left, beside a fire-place is a sofa and an oval table. Beside it a rocking-chair. In the dining-room the richly set table can be seen. Dinner is over and a servant is clearing away the things.* HERR MUHLINGK, FRAU MUHLINGK, KURT *and* LEONORE *are drinking coffee in the drawing-room. The servant who has passed the cups goes out.*

KURT. As I remarked before, the black horse is fine!

Kurt. Expensive it certainly is!

Frau Muhlingk. I shall make up the rest of the money, just to stop the argument.

Kurt. (*Kisses her hand*) My best thanks, Mama;—Now I can show myself to Berlin mounted and spurred!—You can admire me, too, Lori!

Leonore. (*Without looking up from her book*) Yes, my dear.

Kurt. Lothar Brandt and Hugo Stengel wanted to come out to see the beast. Perhaps that doesn't interest you either, Lori?

Leonore. They will probably come often. They haven't anything else to do. (*Looking at the clock—aside*) Oh, how the time drags! (*The servant goes out*)

Frau Muhlingk. You must not speak so harshly about these gentlemen, my child. You know Lothar wants to pay court to you.

Leonore. Really?

Frau Muhlingk. Haven't you noticed it?

Leonore. I haven't paid any particular attention.

Frau Muhlingk. (*To her husband*) It's unbearable, Theodore!

Muhlingk. We've had enough of this tone, my child. Even the pride in your paternal bank account has its limits.

Leonore. (*Looking at him*) Pride in the paternal bank account?

Muhlingk. Well, how can we explain this manner you have assumed for the last ten years, sending home every rich and respected man who has proposed to you?—I am a simple, middle-class man. I made my own way with my own help——

Kurt. That is to say, he married a rich wife.

Muhlingk. What's that, Kurt?

Kurt. An exclamation of admiration, Father; nothing else.

Muhlingk. No, I didn't have it as easy as you,

my boy. You might well follow my example. I
don't like to play the spender and I don't care to
see it in my children, either. That is the only way
one can live tastefully!

KURT. —and cheap, too!

LEONORE. Your accusation doesn't apply to me,
papa.

FRAU MUHLINGK. Will you condescend to give
us an explanation then?

LEONORE. Mama!

FRAU MUHLINGK. (*Nervously*) Well?

LEONORE. (*Rising*) Oh, why can't you let me
work out my own salvation? I am modest enough
—I only ask to be allowed to live my own life.

MUHLINGK. You call that modest? If that is
modest, what is to become of the sanctity of family ties?

FRAU MUHLINGK. (*To her husband*) Do you
hear that? I haven't slept for nights and nights!

LEONORE. Because of me, mama?

FRAU MUHLINGK. Every day these mad ideas,
these unconventional acts! Now what does it
mean this time, when you plunder the hothouse to
send flowers to a clerk!

LEONORE. You mean Robert?

FRAU MUHLINGK. The young Herr Heinecke, I
mean.

LEONORE. He isn't a clerk. He is almost a member of the family!

KURT. Oh, thank you.

FRAU MUHLINGK. (*Mildly*) That is, we brought
him up out of the gutter.

MUHLINGK. (*As the servant enters*) Eh?

WILHELM. The young Herr Heinecke from the
alley sends word that he will take the liberty of——

(LEONORE *looks at the clock involuntarily.*)

MUHLINGK. Well, well—just like a noble gentleman! That is good!

WILHELM. —calling, with your permission. He named another gentleman. Count Trast, or some-one——

MUHLINGK. (*Jumping up*) What! Count Trast! Trast and Company, Kurt! The coffee King. (*Motions the servant off*)

KURT. What luck that clerk has!

MUHLINGK. Oh, we must invite him to the house, Amalie.

FRAU MUHLINGK. Very good,—to-morrow morning.

LEONORE. What! and not invite Robert Hein-ecke too?

KURT. (*Aside*) Better and better!

MUHLINGK. Well, perhaps you are right. When one descends to the level of these people one really unites their interests with the interests of the firm. A thing like that often brings in thousands, Kurt. The young fellow did very well under Benno's direction and inasmuch as I'm thinking of sending him for ten years into the Antilles, I——

LEONORE. (*Indignantly*) Oh, I did not mean it that way, papa!

MUHLINGK. Oh, that's all right.

FRAU MUHLINGK. And, Kurt, you must take care that the young fellow doesn't make any *faux pas*. He comes from the alley, you know. A thing like that might spoil the whole affair.

KURT. (*Standing up*) Pardon me, did you expect I would invite my friends?

MUHLINGK. Certainly, your friends, too! Bachelors always have plenty of time.

KURT. (*Standing up*) Pardon me, I should like to ask to be excused from doing that. I can't be expected to introduce gentlemen of good family to the son of (*Indicating the alley*) Herr Heinecke.

LEONORE. (*Aside*) Would you rather have the brother of Miss Heinecke here?

KURT. (*Shocked, then gathering himself to-gether*) What do you mean?

LEONORE. Be thankful I don't insist on an answer.

KURT. Really!

LEONORE. Shall I?

KURT. So you're threatening me, are you?

MUHLINGK. My dear children, in this house we won't have any scenes, please.

FRAU MUHLINGK. Don't let's pay any attention to it, Theodore. I'll lie down now and rest for a minute or two—Won't you?

(MUHLINGK *kisses her ceremoniously on the fore-head.*)

KURT. (*Aside*) The good old days! Good-bye! (FRAU MUHLINGK *goes towards door.* MUHLINGK *rings*)

LEONORE. (*Hurrying after* FRAU MUHLINGK) Mother!

FRAU MUHLINGK. (*Turns around, speaks nerv-ously, but in a friendly tone*) Never mind! It's all right! (*She goes out*)

MUHLINGK. Ask any visitors to come into my office.

(MUHLINGK *and the* SERVANT *go out.* KURT *also starts to go.*)

LEONORE. It seems to me we have something to say to each other.

KURT. We? Oh, no!

LEONORE. You don't want to draw me into an argument, perhaps?

KURT. It doesn't seem to suit you when I take a notion to see a little of the world. Because you are four years older than I, and because you taught me to walk, you'd still like to have me tied to your apron-strings. You—but I can go—alone now.

There are ladies who have said I go too far. Let
me find heaven in my own way.

LEONORE. I have never interfered with you. Go
on, play the man-of-the world as much as you like,
but have the courage to admit it.

KURT. What good would that do?

LEONORE. You play the dutiful son and then
make fun of your parents behind their backs. Believe me, Kurt; you are ruining your character.

KURT. (*Laughing*) No!

LEONORE. There is just one thing I ask of you
—at least keep this house and its surroundings
sacred.

KURT. We'll do that with the help of the Lord!

LEONORE. Do you know what they are whisper-
ing around the factory? That you are paying far
too much attention to Robert Heinecke's sister—
that you——

KURT. (*Shrugging his shoulders*) Yes, and you
allow yourself to carry the gossip of the backstairs
about——

LEONORE. Kurt, not that tone! I defended you
from Mama aand Papa to-day. The next time I
shan't do it. And remember one thing: Robert has
come back.—If he finds his sister guilty—don't
worry, I wouldn't dare think it!—But the girl is
frivolous and vain! If it *were* so—and you were to
blame, Kurt, take care! He would break you in
pieces!

KURT. Who? My clerk?—with his sample-
case?

LEONORE. And you stoop to steal this from your
clerk.

KURT. What's that? Steal—steal what?

LEONORE. His position in the world! His good
name!

KURT. The good name of Heinecke—bah!

(*Enter a servant with two visiting cards which he
hands to* LEONORE.)

LEONORE. Visitors for you.
KURT. Who?
LEONORE. Read!
KURT. Lothar Brandt.—Hugo Stengel.—Show them in. (*Throws the cards on the table,* SERVANT *goes out*)

(LEONORE *drops into the rocking-chair.*)

KURT. Signs and miracles! You didn't run away.

(*Enter* HUGO STENGEL *and* LOTHAR BRANDT.)

LOTHAR. 'Morning, old fellow.
KURT. (*Going to him*) You've come to see my horse. This is very good of you!
HUGO. (*Bowing to* LENORE) We took the liberty!
LOTHAR. (*Bowing to* LEONORE) If we aren't disturbing the Gnadiges Fraulein.
LEONORE. (*Politely*) Certainly not. I seldom go into the stables.

(BRANDT *and* STENGEL *clear their throats.*)

KURT. Won't you sit down?
LOTHAR. We await the permission of Fraulein Leonore.
LEONORE. (*Coolly*) Oh, please! (*She takes a book and begins turning the leaves.* KURT *throws her a look. They sit down*)
KURT. Well, where were you yesterday?
LOTHAR. (*Affectedly*) Ah, by Jove, you make an awful demand on a man's memory. What was I doing yesterday? First I went riding, then I had a conference with Father.—Coffee is sinking again.
HUGO. Alarmingly—53 and a half.
LOTHAR. Alarmingly, is not the right word. It *is* sinking. We'll make a fight. Then I made

some visits, then I dined at the Officers' Association——

LEONORE. (*Looking up*) Ah, you are an officer?

LOTHAR. (*Insulted*) I thought you knew, Gnadiges Fraulein?—I am a Reserve Lieutenant in the "Crown Prince" Cuirassier regiment.

LEONORE. (*Smiling, looking toward the table*) Ah, yes! Note visiting card!

KURT. (*Slapping him on the back*) And besides that, boots and saddles astride Papa's desk chair.

LOTHAR. (*Sharply*) Oh I say, old fellow!

LEONORE. The desk chair isn't the slowest horse in the race for fortune you know, Herr Lieutenant.

HUGO. Oh, that was good!

KURT. But I looked for you last evening.

LOTHAR. The evening.—We were invited somewhere? Where? It isn't quite clear in my memory now. We won't discuss the matter. You seem to be amused, Gnadiges Fraulein?

LEONORE. Is that forbidden?

LOTHAR. But really, you know, you in your pride and seclusion, have hardly an idea what the word *saison* means in our good German tongue.

HUGO. It is quite two months, Gnadiges Fraulein, that I have done what you might really call sleeping.

KURT. And that was on a billiard table.

LOTHAR. Oh, our respected Kurt meant that as a joke! But if you knew what it meant to be a martyr to amusement, you would understand what we mean.

LEONORE. I have made such an effort to understand you that I already begin to feel sorry for you.

HUGO. (*Aside to* LOTHAR) I believe the girl is making fun of us.

LOTHAR. (*Aside, arrogantly*) Every woman tries to be a coquette.

KURT. (*Who has gone over to* LENORE, *aside*) You don't need to be so disagreeable.

LEONORE. (*Rocking*) Hm? (*Goes on reading*)

LOTHAR. Might I ask what it is that takes so
much of the Gnadiges Fraulein's attention.

KURT. (*To himself*) If he would only let her
be!

LEONORE. Something that would hardly be of interest to the martyrs of amusement—for it concerns
the martyrs of labor.

LOTHAR. Ah, I see.

HUGO. (*Getting up*) But weren't we going to
see the horse?

LOTHAR. Ah yes! you two go ahead—The martyrs of labor interest me more than the Gnadiges
Fraulein believes.

KURT. (*To himself*) Oh, the poor devil!

HUGO. Good heavens!

KURT. Come, Stengel, come! (*They go out*)

LEONORE. (*Looking impatiently at the clock*) In
what way can I be of service to you, Herr Brandt?

LOTHAR. Gnadiges Fraulein, I very much regret
that you quite misunderstand me, for although I admit that I——

LEONORE. And in order to prove that, you are
willing to waste——

LOTHAR. A moment, please!

LEONORE. (*Aside*) A proposal!

LOTHAR. My faults may be without number, but,
Gnadiges Fraulein, I am a man of honor.

LEONORE. I should think that that was to be
taken for granted from the son of a respectable
family, Herr Brandt, and as little worthy of praise
as the fact that he wears a well-cut coat.

LOTHAR. Then you respect honor no more?

LEONORE. Pardon me. I meant no disrespect to
the ill-clad. But one doesn't bring them into the
porlor. But I interrupted you, Herr Brandt. Perhaps I do misunderstand you. Please continue.

LOTHAR. I must admit, Gnadiges Fraulein, you
have intimidated me. And that is something! For
what is a man without courage?

LEONORE. Ah, that is another thing. Courage, I can respect! But what have you done so far that has shown your courage?

LOTHAR. Ask my friends. That at least is above reproach.

LEONORE. In other words, you have fought a duel.

LOTHAR. One doesn't discuss such things before ladies.

LEONORE. But we hear about them just the same. We are here to offer the victor his laurels. Did you ever break a lance in defence of a conviction which you know in your heart you yourself have violated?

LOTHAR. (*Indignantly*) How can you ask that? Such a thing could never occur to me!

LEONORE. Or have you never silently borne an unworthy suspicion?

LOTHAR. I? Silently? On the contrary.

LEONORE. Never?

LOTHAR. Never, Fraulein.

LEONORE. Then one can't be absolutely certain about your courage, Herr—may I say Lieutenant?— (*She rises*) First the test, and then perhaps we can discuss the matter further.

LOTHAR. (*Trying to hold her back*) Fraulein—

(*Enter* WILHELM.)

WILHELM. Will the gentlemen step in here a moment?

LEONORE. At last!

(ROBERT *and the* COUNT *enter;* LENORE *runs to meet* ROBERT.)

TRAST. (*To himself*) So that's the story! (*To the servant who is about to go out*) Here, come here! (*He takes one of the cards from the tray and puts it in his pocket*)

LOTHAR. (*Looking at* ROBERT *and* LEONORE) What does that mean?

TRAST. My card is enough.

(*The servant goes out.*)

ROBERT. Leonore, I've brought Count Trast, my benefactor and my best friend.

LEONORE. (*Remembering* LOTHAR) The gentlemen will permit me to introduce Herr Lothar Brandt? Herr Count von Trast—Herr Robert Heinecke, a playmate of my childhood.

LOTHAR. (*To himself*) She introduces me to Alma's brother—That is fine!—The gentlemen will pardon me, but my friends—(*Stutters and clears his throat*)

TRAST. Are waiting for you, eh?

LOTHAR. (*Staring at him*) Exactly! (*As he goes*) What sort of a count is he? (*Turns at the door and bows stiffly, clicking his heels and goes out*)

LEONORE. You have been away from home a long time, Herr Count?

TRAST. I have inhabited the tropics for a quarter century.

LEONORE. For pleasure?

TRAST. As much as possible. Meanwhile I have been speculator in coffee, cloves and ivory, and elephant-hunter.

LEONORE. (*Laughing*) In which of your many capacities am I to welcome you then, you many-gifted man?

TRAST. You may take your choice, Gnadiges Fraulein.

WILHELM. (*At the door*) The Herr Councillor is at your disposal.

ROBERT. I must——

TRAST. (*To* ROBERT) Stay where you are. I have something to say to the manager first. (*To* LEONORE) For ten years, he has been singing your praises; shouldn't you take the trouble to listen to ten minutes' praise of me?

LEONORE. (*Shaking her finger at* TRAST) You are an old rogue!

TRAST. A rogue in your own service! (*He goes out*)

LEONORE. (*Taking* ROBERT'S *hand*) At last I have you here again!

ROBERT. I thank you from the bottom of my heart for those words.

LEONORE. Oh, how polite we are!—My words aren't alms! Come here. (*Leads him to the fireplace*) Sit down—here by the fire—beside me. You mustn't freeze in cold Germany!—Wait, I'll start up the fire! (*She blows with the bellows*) These fireplaces are—impractical things—most impractical, but anyway we can chat in front of it. In India you don't need fireplaces, do you? (*To herself*) I'm so happy!—Oh, I'm glad to see you again. And now, out with the "but" that you have up your sleeve. I'll parry it.

ROBERT. Don't make my heart too heavy.

LEONORE. That's the last thing I want to do.

ROBERT. But that's what you're doing when you conjure up this ghost of a happiness that is now forever buried.

LEONORE. Oh, if you were only as you used to be.

ROBERT. So I am, Heaven knows!—but there is a gulf between us!

LEONORE. Then there was—yes!

ROBERT. God!—you must understand me! I cana't say what's in my heart—do you remember what you said to me when we parted?

LEONORE. Well?

ROBERT. You said: "Be true to me, Robert."

LEONORE. Is that what I said? Exactly that?

ROBERT. Such a thing one doesn't forget.

LEONORE. They had forbidden us to call each other by our first names.

ROBERT. But you did it just the same.

LEONORE. And why don't we do it any more?

ROBERT. You are playing with me.

LEONORE. You are right, my friend. And I must not do it. It would look like coquetry, although it is nothing but the joy of seeing you again. You have shown me plainly enough that the dream of our childhood is over.

ROBERT. It must be. Your father lifted me out of the gutter in a moment of overflowing generosity. Everything that I think and know and feel I must thank him for. And for that very reason I have lost the right of independent action. I am a dependent of this house, and have not the right to approach its young mistress—in any way whatever.

LEONORE. Your own pride punishes your lying words!

ROBERT. Perhaps it is my pride that forces me to accept this position!

LEONORE. And you are not willing to sacrifice a little of it for my sake?

ROBERT. Don't torture me! It isn't that alone! Only think what I am suffering. For the first time, this moment, when I sit opposite you, do I realize anything like a home-coming! But I would be terribly selfish if I allowed myself to admit this feeling. Back there in the alley is my family!—Father, mother, sister—and this family—is my family! Oh, I tell you things have happened back there that you in your goodness can't even imagine.

LEONORE. My dear friend, one doesn't have to go to India to become estranged from one's family.

ROBERT. You, too?

LEONORE. It is better not to speak of it. I am ashamed of myself. I am even more of an outcast than you. I have lost all sense of duty. A sort of gloomy ill-will has come over me and now it is almost arrogance—towards my own people and all the others about them—aand I'm not arrogant or proud by nature! Tell me, what is it that——?

ROBERT. Shh!

(TRAST *and* MUHLINGK *enter at the right.*)

MUHLINGK. (*To* TRAST) Well, until to-morrow then, Count.—Ah, there is the young man. (*Extending his hand*) Welcome, welcome, do you want to go ver the report at once?

ROBERT. I only came to present my respects, Herr Councillor, my papers aren't unpacked yet.

MUHLINGK. Well, well, there's no hurry. But what are you doing here, Leonore?

LEONORE. I simply wanted to say how d'ye do to Robert.

MUHLINGK. Mm—But you know that Mama has been asking for you. Come, young man, I have plans for you; plans. You know, Count, we have no secrets from you.

TRAST. You can get to know him better if you are alone with him. (*To* ROBERT) I'll wait for you here.

LEONORE. (*Shaking* ROBERT'S *hand*) Au revoir, Robert.

MUHLINGK. Hm! (*Reprovingly. He goes out with* ROBERT)

LEONORE. Count, you heard—? I must go.

TRAST. Gnadiges Fraulein! (LEONORE *goes to door, he watches her, she turns and he shakes his finger at her*)

LEONORE. (*Surprised*) What do you mean, Count?

TRAST. Hm—I mean! (*He claps his hands*)

LEONORE. And what does that mean?

TRAST. That means—(*Through his hands*) Bravo!

LEONORE. (*Dignified*) I don't understand you, Count—ah! (*She bursts out laughing and goes up frankly and puts out her hand*)   Yes, I do understand.

TRAST.   (*Taking her hand in both his*)   That's better.

LEONORE.   Count!

TRAST.   Fraulein!   (LEONORE *goes out*)   She's a splendid specimen—that girl!   I'll let her have him. He must have her.

(*Enter* KURT.)

KURT.   (*To* STENGEL *who is coming in*)   Courage, courage, my boy!   Come in.

TRAST.   (*Recognizing* KURT *as he comes in with* BRANDT)   He—here!

KURT.   (*Sees* TRAST; *startled, goes up to him, in a low voice*)   You wished to see me, sir?

TRAST.   No, but I'm glad to see you.

KURT.   With whom have I the honor——?

TRAST.   Count Trast.

KURT.   (*Astonished and very polite*)   Ah, we may thank—thank—our employe—er—our—a traveling acquaintanceship, I suppose—for this visit?

TRAST.   You are the son of the house?

KURT.   I beg your pardon, yes!   At your service! Naturally—ah, Count, we are both men-of-the world enough to forget the affair of last night.

TRAST.   You think so?

KURT.   The girl is nice, I ought to know if anyone does.   All honor to your good taste.   But you must admit that I was in the right.   I hope there will be no rivalry?

TRAST.   Especially, as the girl's brother is the best friend I have?

KURT.   (*Frightened, controls himself, then, after a pause*)   What do you intend to do?

TRAST.   I have not decided as yet.   If I can dissuade him from his imaginary duties to your house, and if I find you prepared to break off all further relationship, then perhaps I can remain silent.

KURT. And otherwise?

TRAST. That would be a matter for Herr Heinecke to settle.

KURT. Do you think I would accept a challenge from my clerk?

TRAST. Your what?—Oh, I see.

KURT. Count, do what you please.

TRAST. That is a habit of mine. Herr Heinecke is at this moment in your father's office. Permit me to remain here a few minutes in order that I may shorten your meeting. I should like to prevent you two from shaking hands.

KURT. The room is yours, Count.

TRAST. I thank you. (*They separate, and* TRAST *looks at the pictures.* KURT *walks excitedly away from the others*)

LOTHAR. (*To* HUGO) What happened between those two? If I remember rightly there was a Count Trast in our regiment who came to a bad end. Wait a moment.

HUGO. (*Nervously*) You aren't going to start a quarrel?

LOTHAR. Why not? The other fellow has some scheme. (*He approaches* TRAST) The Count seems to like solitude.

TRAST. (*Turning*) Decidedly!

LOTHAR. That is rather impolite.

TRAST. (*Looking at him squarely*) Ah! you seem to be carrying your sense of honor on your shoulder, Herr—er—pardon!

LOTHAR. My name is Lothar Brandt and I feel that it is necessary to add that I am Lieutenant of the Reserves in the Cuirassier Regiment "Crown Prince."

TRAST. (*Politely*) Is that all?

LOTHAR. (*Threateningly*) Is that all, Count?

TRAST. Pardon me! One serves in the Reserves during war time only. When I came back I hoped that I could live in peace.

LOTHAR. You are mistaken, Count, one serves in the Reserves during the rifle practice, as well.

TRAST. Do you need me for rifle practice?

LOTHAR. Permit me, Count, to ask you a question.

TRAST. With pleasure.

LOTHAR. In the regiment to which it is my great honor to belong there was formerly a young fellow who bore the same name as yours.

TRAST. Ah? Then it was probably I.

LOTHAR. (*Sharply*) The man left the army under a cloud.

TRAST. Exactly! Exactly! (*Very polite*) And if you wish to say in other words, that when we meet on the street you don't care to recognize me—I release you from the necessity of greeting—I can do without it. (*Bows and picks up a portfolio which he examines*)

HUGO. (*Enthusiastically*) Well, *I* was never despatched as elegantly as that. (*He approaches* TRAST *and bows deeply*)—Permit me—my·name is Stengel!

TRAST. (*Turning*) Charmed!

HUGO. Stengel! (TRAST *bows—they talk*)

KURT. (*Comes forward and joins* LOTHAR) Man, what are you trying to do. That's the almighty firm of Trast and Company.--Do you want to ruin your father's business?

LOTHAR. (*Dismayed*) Why didn't you tell me before?

KURT. Whatever happens we must straighten the matter out.

LOTHAR. If you can do it in perfectly good form.

KURT. Pardon me, Count—my friend regrets——

LOTHAR. Regrets is hardly the word, Kurt.

KURT. (*Stuttering*) Well—er—er——

TRAST. Perhaps our friend would like to consider our little conversation as not having taken place?

LOTHAR. We can go as far as that at least, Kurt.

TRAST. I must keep pace with his generosity, and—express the same desire.

KURT. Then the matter is settled.

LOTHAR. And I take the liberty to express my pleasure at meeting personally, the man whose work I have respected for so many years.

TRAST. (*Very politely*) You see, Lieutenant, that it was not entirely superfluous when I asked "Is that all?" As business men, we can understand each other perfectly. Gentlemen, Herr Brandt Junior, heir to the worthy firm of importers, Brandt and Stengel, with which I am pleased to have business relations, has just given me a little statement in private on the theme of "Honor." Permit me to make the answer public. (*They sit down*) In confidence, there is no such thing as honor. (*All are astonished*) Don't be frightened. It won't hurt you.

LOTHAR. And what we call honor?

TRAST. What we commonly call honor is nothing more than the shadow we throw in the sunlight of publicity. But the worst part of it is that we have as many kinds of honor as we have business circles and strata. How can one find his way among them?

LOTHAR. (*Sharply*) You are mistaken, Count. There is only one honor, just as there is only one sun and one God. One must feel that—or he is no gentleman.

TRAST. Hm!—Permit me to tell you a little tale. In a journey through Central Asia I stopped at the house of a Thibetan Chief. I was dusty and footsore. He received me, sitting on his throne. Beside him was his charming little wife. "Rest yourself, traveler," he said to me, "my wife will prepare you a bath and then we men shall dine together." And he gave me over to his young wife.—Gentlemeen, if ever in my life my self-control was put to test it was in that hour—And when I returned to

the hall, what did I find? The attendants under
arms, threatening voices and half-drawn swords.
" You must die! " cried my host, " you have given a
deadly insult to the honor of my house. You have
scorned to accept the most sacred thing I could offer
you."—You see, gentlemen, I am still living, for
eventually the deficient sense of honor of the bar-
baric European was forgiven. (*They laugh*) If
you happen to know any of our modern writers on
the theme of adultery you might tell them this
story.

(*All laugh, and move gradually towards the left.*)

TRAST. (*Continuing*) Gentlemen, I don't want
to be considered immoral. The study of the puzzles
of civilization is a thing apart.—You see it lies in
the nature of your so-called honor, that it may only
be possessed by the certain few, the demi-gods; for
it is an emotional luxury that loses value in direct
proportion as it is appropriated by the rabble.

KURT. But that is a paradox, Count. Is it not
permitted to everyone to be a man of honor?

TRAST. On the contrary. Then the poorest devil
in the alley might dispute the honor of a gentleman. (KURT *is perplexed*)

LOTHAR. If he acts according to honor, then he
must be a gentleman.

TRAST. Hm! Really? May I tell you another,
a shorter story?—But I am afraid I'm boring you.

LOTHAR *and* HUGO. (*Laughing*) No!—No!

TRAST. It took place somewhere in South Amer-
ica—the Spaniards are the aristocrats there,—the
population is a mixture of negroes, Indians, and a
sort of white trash. A product of this mixed race,
—his name was—hm—Pepe—had the opportunity
of being transported to the Spanish mother country
where he (*Breathes on his left elbow*) absorbed a
little of the pure Castillan sense of honor. (ROBERT
enters without being heard and listens) When he

came back, after several years, he found his little
sister on all too intimate terms with a young aristocrat—Gentleman, we mustn't get angry. Considering her origin it was the girl's destiny. But the
young fellow dared to attempt to avenge his sister's
honor, not as a mestizo but as a Hidalgo!

KURT. (*In a hurt voice*) Listen, that means me!

TRAST. You see, gentlemen, that was madness
and he was treated as a madman. Then the fellow
showed his real nature. Like a thug he waited for
the young nobleman and he shot him down. He
was sentenced, and even under the very gallows the
fool declared,—his name was Pepe—that he was
dying for his honor. Gentlemen, isn't that absurd?

ROBERT. (*Who has made his appearance unob-
served*) You are mistaken, my friend! This fool
was right. I should have acted exactly the same
way.

TRAST. Oh, oh, it's you! (*Going quickly to him*)
You don't know these people! Don't look around.
Come with me. (*Draws him toward the door*)

ROBERT. Isn't that Kurt?

TRAST. They are strangers.—Come. You will
excuse me, gentlemen? We are in a hurry. Good-
bye.

LOTHAR. (*To* KURT) Now, I'll settle him. (*To*
TRAST) Permit me just one more question, Count.
(*Affectedly*) If you intend to do away with honor
entirely; what do you expect gentlemen of honor to
put in its place?

TRAST. (*Straightening up*) Duty, young man—
(*To himself*) This is certainly unpleasant, Gentlemen——

KURT. (*As* TRAST *and* ROBERT *are about to
leave*) It was a great honor to our house, Count.

ROBERT. Pardon me, but you are Herr Kurt
Muhlingk?

KURT. That is my name?

ROBERT. (*Confused*) But—aren't—? Of course,

you don't recognize me! I am—(*He is about to offer his hand to* KURT)

TRAST. (*Stepping between*) You don't shake hands with this man.

ROBERT. (*Looks about confused, stares at* KURT, *then at* TRAST, *then at* KURT *again, gives a little cry, then controls himself*) I should like to have a word with you—Herr Muhlingk—in private.

KURT. As you see, I have some guests here now, but in an hour I shall be at your service.

ROBERT. In an hour, Herr Muhlingk!

TRAST. (*To himself*) He found out quickly enough!

(TRAST *and* ROBERT *go to the door as*

THE CURTAIN FALLS.)

ACT III.

SCENE:—*The same as in Act I. A lamp is burning on the table. Daylight is coming through the window. Up-stage to the left is a bed, turned down. It has not been slept in.* ROBERT *sits at the table his face in his hands.*

(*Enter* FRAU HEINECKE *in night-cap and wearing a woollen under-skirt.*)

FRAU HEINECKE. Good-morning, my son! (*He does not answer*) Poor thing! he ain't even been to bed! (*Goes to him, wiping her eyes*) Bobby!

ROBERT. (*Starts up*) What is it? What do you want?

FRAU HEINECKE. Lord, how you yell at me! And your teeth are chattering with cold! Won't you drink some coffee? (*He shakes his head decisively*) Take a little piece of advice from your old mother,

Bobby; even if a person is in trouble, he's got to
sleep. Sleep puts marrow in the bones. (*Puts out
the lamp*)

ROBERT. Mother, Mother, what have you done?

FRAU HEINECKE. (*Crying*) We aren't to blame,
my boy!

ROBERT. Not to blame!

FRAU HEINECKE. I brought her up honorably.
There has never been a bad example in this house.
I kept her at her schooling and I had her confirmed,
though that ain't even necessary any more. She
went up to the altar in a new black pleated dress. I
bought it myself at a bargain, and I put my own
wedding handkerchief into her hand, and the
preacher spoke so movin', so movin'.

ROBERT. But how could you allow her to have
anything to do with that—fellow!

FRAU HEINECKE. Perhaps it wasn't really so
bad——

ROBERT. What further proof do you want?
Didn't he admit everything to me with the most
brutal frankness? Or did Alma try to lie about it?
And to cap the climax, last evening I was in
Michalski's house. Everything was beautifully arranged. Your dear daughter Auguste had prepared
a secret nest, with curtains and carpets and red
hanging lamps. She kept watch at the door herself and was—paid, paid for it! The cur was in my
hands yesterday. If I had only finished him then!

FRAU HEINECKE. Why, Robert——

ROBERT. Be still! He promised satisfaction. I
accomplished that much at least. He saw I was
ready for anything. He said he would find means
of giving me satisfaction by to-day. I thought of
the poor little girl's future and let him go.

FRAU HEINECKE. Well, I never suspected anything wrong.

ROBERT. You must have seen it coming. What

did you think when he brought her home so late at night?

FRAU HEINECKE. When a person is asleep, he's glad enough he don't have to think. Besides, she had a latchkey.

ROBERT. But you couldn't neglect the fact that if he brought her home he must have met her somewhere in the city.

FRAU HEINECKE. Well, yes. I thought she was *going* with him.

ROBERT. I don't know what you mean.

FRAU HEINECKE. She was *going* with him.

ROBERT. So you said, but I——

FRAU HEINECKE. Just like any young girl goes with a young gentleman.

ROBERT. Goes? Where?

FRAU HEINECKE. To concerts, to restaurants— If he's got money, to the theater, and in summer to Grunewald * or Treptow.*

ROBERT. Alone?

FRAU HEINECKE. Alone? (*Clacks her tongue*) No! With the young man!

ROBERT. I meant: without her parents?

FRAU HEINECKE. Certainly. Or do you expect the old mother is going to toddle after the young ones on her weak legs.

ROBERT. Mm! So you knew she " went " with him?

FRAU HEINECKE. No, I just thought so.

ROBERT. And when you asked her?

FRAU HEINECKE. Why should I ask? That would only be wasting breath. A girl ought to know herself what's good for her.

ROBERT. Oh!

FRAU HEINECKE. But that she—oh, who'd have thought it! Lord, how you tremble. I must get this room warm for you. (*Goes to stove*)

*Suburbs of Berlin.—Tr.

ROBERT. (*To himself*) No way out! No way
to save things! Shame!—a life of shame!

FRAU HEINECKE. (*Into the kitchen*) Father,
bring in some coke! (*Kneels and shakes down the
fire*)

ROBERT. (*To himself*) What sort of satisfaction can he have meant? Marriage? (*He laughs*)
And if it came to that, I'm not sure whether I
should want marriage for her. At least there is the
chance of a duel. If he shoots me down, then I'm
saved. But—what will become of these? (*Gesture*)

(*Enter* HEINECKE *in a torn dressing-gown, and
large felt slippers, he carries a basket of coke.*)

HEINECKE. (*Gruffly*) Good-morning.

ROBERT. Good-morning, Father.

HEINECKE. (*Muttering*) Yes, yes——

FRAU HEINECKE. Quit grumbling, Father. Help
me make a fire.

HEINECKE. Yes—Yes, we'll make a fire. (*They
both kneel before the stove*)

ROBERT. (*To himself*) And if I kill him? I'll
admit that would be a relief! But the question remains: what will become of them? *Looking toward
his parents*) I'm afraid that I can't afford the luxury of a sense of honor. (*Crying out*) Oh, how
vile I am!

HEINECKE. Something wrong, my boy?

FRAU HEINECKE. It's because of Alma. He
hasn't even been to bed.

HEINECKE. Yes, Alma! That's what a man
grows gray in honor for. But I always said it: the
Avenue'll bring us trouble some day.

FRAU HEINECKE. (*To* HEINECKE) Father,
don't cry! (*They embrace*)

ROBERT. (*To himself*) But someone's heart
must break!

HEINECKE. Oh, I'm not crying! I'm master of
this house! I know what I've got to do! Poor
cripple has his honor, too. Think I'll stand for it!
My daughter! She'll see! (*Swinging the poker*)
I'll give her my curse! My paternal curse!

FRAU HEINECKE. (*Arranging the bed*) Now,
now, now——

HEINECKE. Yes, you! You don't understand
anything about honor. (*Strikes his breast*) There
lies honor! Out into the streets she'll go! Out into
the night and the storm!

ROBERT. Do you want her to be absolutely
ruined?

FRAU HEINECKE. Let him talk, he don't mean
anything.

ROBERT. Won't you see where she is? I suppose
she's ashamed to show herself.

FRAU HEINECKE. She wanted to sleep.

ROBERT. Oh!

FRAU HEINECKE. (*She goes to the bed-room
door*) Alma! (*No answer*)

ROBERT. Oh, she never should have been left
alone.

FRAU HEINECKE. (*Opens the door*) Just as I
said, she's asleep.

ROBERT. She can sleep!

FRAU HEINECKE. Will you get up, you worthless
girl?

HEINECKE. Come, get up, or there'll be trouble.

ROBERT. Father, Mother, quick, before she
comes! Don't be too hard with her. It will only
make her more stubborn.

FRAU HEINECKE. You are a good deal more
clever than your old mother, but just the same I
know how to take care of my children. I'll keep her
like in a reform-school if it breaks my heart:—
cleaning boots, peeling potatoes, cleaning floors,
scrubbing steps, she's got to do it all.

ROBERT. And suppose she runs away some night?

HEINECKE. Pah, she'll be locked up. I'll have the key in my pocket. How'll she run away then?

ROBERT. But think, she is only a child! And the rest are more to blame than she. Her own sister—Ah, if you want to be severe you ought to be severe with that damned procuress!—I hope I can demand once for all that Alma be taken absolutely away from under the influence of her sister and that you'll show Auguste and her husband the door!

HEINECKE. Certainly, we'll make a clean sweep of that outfit. I've had enough of Michalski. Now you see, Mother, Robert has to come all the way from India to say it! You haven't any respect for me, poor old man!

ROBERT. I beg your pardon, Father—this doesn't concern you.

HEINECKE. Just the same——

FRAU HEINECKE. (*Her apron over her face*) But she is my child, too! And I love all my children the same!

ROBERT. Even if they aren't worthy of your love?

FRAU HEINECKE. Then all the more.

ROBERT. Shh!

(ALMA *appears in the bed-room door dressed in a nightgown and a white underskirt, her hair is down and she looks fearfully from one to the other.*)

HEINECKE. Hoho!

FRAU HEINECKE. (*Wringing her hands*) Child! child, is this our reward? Haven't I done everything in the world for you? Haven't I kept you like a princess? But now it's over. What are you standing there for? Get a broom! Sweep the room!

(ALMA *slips past her with her elbows up, as if fearing a blow, into the kitchen.*)

HEINECKE. (*Walking excitedly up and down*)

I'm your poor old father and I tell you I brought
you into the world!—Yes, an honest old man!
That I am!

(ALMA *appears in the kitchen door with broom and
dustpan.*)

ROBERT. (*To himself*) How sweet she looks in
her penitence! and she——

FRAU HEINECKE. Well, are you going to begin?

HEINECKE. (*Ceremoniously*) Alma, my daughter, come here—close!

ALMA. Please, please, don't strike me.

HEINECKE. That is the least I'll do! I'm an
honest old man! Yes, here lies honor! Do you
know what I'm going to do with you now? I'm
going to curse you! What do you say to that?

ALMA. Go away—let me alone.

HEINECKE. You defy me, do you?—you don't
know me yet! you!

FRAU HEINECKE. Father, be still! she's got to
work.

HEINECKE. What! I can't be allowed to curse
my own disobedient child.

FRAU HEINECKE. Oh, that only happens in
books!

HEINECKE. Hey?

ROBERT. My dear parents! You mustn't go on
like this! Please leave me alone with her a moment.
Meanwhile, dress. I daresay there will be visitors.

HEINECKE. And I'm not allowed to curse my—
Hmm, wait!

(FRAU HEINECKE *pulls him out of the room.*)

ROBERT. (*To himself*) Now I'll see what she
really thinks, and what I have to do! (*Softly*)
Come here, sister.

ALMA. Mother said I had to clean the room.

ROBERT. That can wait! (*Takes her hand*) You
don't need to be afraid I won't strike you! And I

won't curse you, either. You may be sure you have one good friend who is willing to keep watch over you—a true and considerate friend.

ALMA. You are too good—Much too good! (*She sinks down before him weeping*)

ROBERT. There, there—get up! Sit on the foot-stool!—There—(*She sits on the stool*) and straighten up, so I can see your eyes. (*Tries to lift her head, but she hides it in her lap*) You won't! Well, cry then! I won't send you away from here —and you will cry for many a day and many a night when you really understand what you have done! Tell me, you realize, don't you, that all the rest of your life must be repentance?

ALMA. Yes, I know.

ROBERT. (*Takes her head in his hands*) Yes, yes, sister, and this is what a man works ten years in a foreign country to build up a fortune for—Ten long years! and twenty will hardly be enough to make us forget this disgrace——

ALMA. In twenty years I'll be old.

ROBERT. Old?—What difference does that make? For us two there is no more youth.

ALMA. Oh, God!

ROBERT. (*Springing up in excitement*) Don't be afraid, we'll stay together! We'll find some hiding place; like hunted animals! Yes, that's what we are! We've been hunted and mangled! (ALMA *sinks down, her face in the empty chair*) Only we two can heal each other's wounds! You mine, and I yours. (*To himself*) Oh, how she lies there! God in Heaven, there is only one thing to do!—the pure little child-soul he has trampled into the dirt, he can never give back—other satisfaction I don't need!—Alma!

ALMA. (*Sitting up*) What?

ROBERT. You really love him?

ALMA. Whom?

ROBERT. Whom? Him!

ALMA. Oh, yes.

ROBERT. And if you lost him entirely, would you feel that you could not bear it at all?

ALMA. Oh no!

ROBERT. Good!—You are a brave little girl!— One can learn to forget!—One can learn—(*He sits down*) Above all, you must work! The singing nonsense is over, of course! You have learned dressmaking, you can begin that again! But you mustn't go back into a shop. There are too many temptations and bad examples there!

ALMA. Yes, yes, the girls are bad.

ROBERT. Let him among you who is without sin—you know! And least of all, you! Where we shall go I can't say as yet. I couldn't think of up-rooting our old parents; otherwise I should take them along. It doesn't matter where—only a long, long way, where you will belong only to me and your work—For you can take my word for it all— tired is half-happy!—Mother and Father would live with us, and you shall help me to take care of them. Besides your dressmaking, you'll have to wash and cook. Will you do that and be patient with Father and Mother?

ALMA. If you want me to.

ROBERT. No, you must want to with a good will, otherwise it is useless. I ask you again, will you?

ALMA. Yes, from to-morrow on, I'll do every-thing.

ROBERT. That's right—but why from to-morrow and not from to-day?

ALMA. Because to-day I was——

ROBERT. Well, well?

ALMA. Oh, please——

ROBERT. (*Kindly*) Out with it!

ALMA. I wanted—to—go—so bad—to the masked ball! (*There is a long pause,* ROBERT *gets up and paces the room*) May I?

ALMA. May I?

ROBERT. Call father and mother.

ALMA. Why not? (*Whining*) Just once! Can't a person have just one good time, if it's to be the last of everything.

ROBERT. Do you know what you're saying?—You——

ALMA. (*Arrogantly*) Yes, I do know what I'm saying! I'm not such a little fool! I know a few things about life myself—What are you so excited about, anyway? Isn't it a pretty hard lot when a person has to sit here for nothing? The sun never shines in an old hole like this, nor the moon either, and all you hear on every side is jabbering and scolding!—and nobody with any decent manners. Father scolds, and mother scolds—and you sew your fingers bloody!—and you get fifty pfennigs a day and that don't even pay for the kerosene!—and when you are young and pretty—and you want to have a good time and go in decent society a little—I was always in favor of something higher—I always liked to read about it in the stories. And as for getting married? Who should I marry, then? Such plebeians as those that work down there in the factory don't interest me! No siree! All they can do is drink up their pay and come home and beat you!—I want a gentleman and if I can't have one I don't want anybody! And Kurt has always treated me decently—I never learned any dirty words from him, I'll tell you—I've picked them up right here at home! And I'm not going to stay here, either! And I don't need you to take care of me, either! Girls like me don't starve to death!

ROBERT. (*Starts to speak then stops*) Call Father and mother!

ALMA. And now I'm going to ask father if I—(*As he threatens her*) Yes, yes, I'm going! (*She goes out*)

ROBERT. So that is the way it stands?—That's my sister! Ah, what a weak fool I was!—Began to

sugar this indecency with poetry and sorrow!—
That wasn't seduction—it was in the blood!—Well,
I must act, now! Rough if need be, otherwise
everything is lost.

(*Enter* FRAU HEINECKE, *pushing* ALMA *before her,*
HEINECKE *follows, his mouth full.*)

HEINECKE.   This impudence!
FRAU HEINECKE.   Masked balls cost money.
Now, you'll stay at home.
HEINECKE.   Do you deserve my curse or not? I
curse you again, you toad!
ROBERT.   Alma, go into the other room! I have
something to say to father and mother.
FRAU HEINECKE.   And don't slop around so!
Dress yourself! The gray dress with the patches!
ALMA.   That old thing!
HEINECKE.   Get out!
FRAU HEINECKE.   And you won't drink any
coffee, either! Now, now, don't cry! (*Aside*) It's
on the back of the stove.

(ALMA *goes out.*)

ROBERT.   Father, Mother,—don't be angry with
me—I—you—there must be a great change in your
life.
HEINECKE.   What's the matter?
ROBERT.   I am certain that Alma will be absolutely ruined if she is not brought into surroundings
that make it impossible for her to return to her
previous life.—But what will become of you? You
can't stay here. If you did, you would soon be a
prey to the Michalskis. So the long and short of it
is—you must come with me.
FRAU HEINECKE.   (*Frightened*) To India?
ROBERT.   It makes no difference where. Perhaps

even as far as India. Trast's influence reaches a long way. We are in a position to choose.

HEINECKE. (*Defiantly*) Oh yes, choose India!

FRAU HEINECKE. I don't know which end I'm on!

ROBERT. It will be hard for you! I realize that. But don't worry; it's not as bad as it seems. You can live a thousand times more comfortably in the tropics than here. You can have as many servants as you like!

HEINECKE. Thousands!

ROBERT. And your own house!

HEINECKE. And palms?

ROBERT. More than you can use.

HEINECKE. And you can pick the fruit right off the trees.

ROBERT. It picks itself.

HEINECKE. And it costs nothing.

ROBERT. Almost nothing.

HEINECKE. And the parrots fly around—and the apes? Like out at the zoo?

ROBERT. So you will come?

FRAU HEINECKE. What do you think, Father?

HEINECKE. Well—'s far's I'm concerned, we'll come.

ROBERT. Thank you, thank you! (*Aside*) Thank God, I didn't have to force them! And now we mustn't lost a moment. Where is paper and pen?

(HEINECKE *meditatively scratches his head.*)

FRAU HEINECKE. Alma has some. (*She goes into bedroom*)

HEINECKE. Of course, she's always writing letters. (*He shuts the stove door*)

ROBERT. (*To himself with a sigh of relief*) Oh, now I'm doubly curious to know what satisfaction he'll offer—and I shall have to refuse! Refuse a duel!—They'll call me a coward and I'll be dis-

honored! Oh, well, I don't need their honor, I
have to earn my bread.

FRAU HEINECKE. (*Entering*) Everything is
laid out on the table—or do you want to write here?

ROBERT. No, no, I shan't be disturbed in there.

FRAU HEINECKE. You look tired. You must
rest a little!

ROBERT. (*Shakes his head*) If Herr Muhlingk,
Junior, sends word, or comes himself, call me. (*He
goes off*)

FRAU HEINECKE. (*Sinking to the chair*) India!

HEINECKE. Drag us old folks half round the
world!

FRAU HEINECKE. Lord Almighty!

HEINECKE. What is it?

FRAU HEINECKE. Michalskis!

HEINECKE. What? Them! (*Buttons his coat*)
They'd better come!

(*A knock is heard.*)

BOTH. (*Quietly*) Come in!

(*Enter* MICHALSKI *and* AUGUSTE.)

MICHALSKI. Morning!

FRAU HEINECKE. Shh!

HEINECKE. (*Threatening with his fist*) You—
you two—get out of here!

AUGUSTE. (*Sitting down*) It's right cold this
morning!

MICHALSKI. (*Sits down and uncorks a bottle*)
Here's a bottle of liqueur I've brought you. Extra
fine—Get me a corkscrew.

FRAU HEINECKE. Some other time! We have
orders to throw you out the door!

AUGUSTE. Who said so?

FRAU HEINECKE. Shh! Robert!

AUGUSTE. What? You let him order you around
in your own house.

HEINECKE. (*In an undertone*) Shh! he's in the bedroom there.

AUGUSTE. (*Pityingly*) Poor father! He's trembling with fear!

MICHALSKI. The idea of frightening two honest people like that! The scoundrel!

FRAU HEINECKE. He ain't a scoundrel! He's a good boy and he's going to take care of us!

HEINECKE. Even if he does want us to go to India!

BOTH. What! Where?

FRAU HEINECKE. To India.

AUGUSTE. What for ⁏

FRAU HEINECKE. Just because Alma wanted to go to a masked ball.

MICHALSKI. Crazy!

FRAU HEINECKE. The few pieces of furniture that made the home so friendly we've got to leave 'em all behind.

AUGUSTE. (*Sentimentally*) And poor me, are you going to leave me, too?—Are you going to sell 'em?

FRAU HEINECKE. The furniture? (AUGUSTE *nods*) We'll have to.

AUGUSTE. The mirror and chairs, too? (FRAU HEINECKE *nods—With feeling*) If I was in your place, instead of selling them for a song, I'd give them to your daughter you're leaving behind. Then you'd be sure they'd be in good hands!

FRAU HEINECKE. (*Looking at her suspiciously, then confidentially, to her husband*) Father! she wants the arm-chairs already.

AUGUSTE. (*Returning to the subject*) Or if you will sell 'em, we would always be the ones to pay the highest, just to keep them in the family.

HEINECKE. But we ain't gone yet.

MICHALSKI. If I was in your place——

FRAU HEINECKE. What'll we do? Now, we're absolutely dependent on him! When he orders, we've got to obey, or else we're put on your hands.

AUGUSTE. We haven't enough to eat for ourselves.

(A knock is heard. Enter COUNCILLOR MUHLINGK. *All start up frightened.)*

MUHLINGK. Good-morning, my people. Is your son at home?

HEINECKE. *(Humbly)* Yes, sir.

FRAU HEINECKE. *(Opening the door)* Robert! *(Tenderly)* Oh, the dear boy, he's falleen asleep in his chair! He didn't sleep a wink all night—Bobby! The Herr Councillor—He's sound asleep!

MUHLINGK. *(Kindly)* Ah? so much the better! Don't wake him.

HEINECKE. Shut the door!

FRAU HEINECKE. But didn't he say——

HEINECKE. —If the young Herr Muhlingk came, he said—*(He shuts the door quietly)*

AUGUSTE. *(To* MICHALSKI, *with gesture of counting money)* Watch!

MUHLINGK. *(Who has been looking around the room)* You seem to be living in a very comfortable place, my good people.

HEINECKE. *(Deferentially)* Would the Herr Councillor be so kind as to sit down?

MUHLINGK. Ha! ha! real silk.

FRAU HEINECKE. Yes, it is silk.

MUHLINGK. A present, perhaps?

FRAU HEINECKE. *(Hesitatingly)* Well, yes, you might say——

MUHLINGK. *(Innocently)* From my son?

HEINECKE. Yes, sir. } *(Together)*
FRAU HEINECKE. Sh! }

MUHLINGK. *(Aside)* Rascal! *(Aloud)* By the way, your good son has not acted in a very dutiful manner toward mine. Frankly, I expected a little more gratitude. You can tell him that he is discharged and that I shall give him until four this afternoon to settle his accounts.

FRAU HEINECKE. Oh, that will make him feel bad.

HEINECKE. He loved the Herr Councillor like his own father!

MUHLINGK. Really! I'm glad to hear it! But that is not what brought me here, good people; you have a daughter.

AUGUSTE. (*Advancing*) At your service!

MUHLINGK. What can I do for you?

AUGUSTE. (*Deferentially*) I am the daughter.

MUHLINGK. Ah, very good, very good. But I was not referring to you. The girl's name is Alma.

FRAU HEINECKE. That's it. And a mighty pretty girl, if I do say it myself.

MUHLINGK. Ah! it is always pleasing to see children who make their parents happy. But there is one thing that I don't like—your daughter has taken advantage of the fact that I have allowed you to occupy my house, and has established illicit relations with my son. Frankly, I expected a little more gratitude.

FRAU HEINECKE. Oh, Herr Councillor!

MUHLINGK. In order to sever all connection whatsoever between your house and mine, I offer you a cash compensation—which you, my dear Heinecke, and your daughter Alma, may divide, with the understanding that half will go to her as a dowry, as soon as she finds someone who—(*Laughs discreetly*) Well, you understand! Until then, the entire sum will be at your disposal. Do you agree?

AUGUSTE. (*Behind* HEINECKE) Say yes!

HEINECKE. I—I——

MUHLINGK. I have offered an unusually large amount in order to free myself of a promise extracted yesterday by your son from my son.—It amounts to—a—fifty thousand marks.

HEINECKE. (*With an exclamation*) God! Herr Councillor, are you in earnest?

FRAU HEINECKE. I'm getting dizzy! (*Sinks into a chair*)

MUHLINGK. (*Aside*) I made it too high!—I put the question again, will you be satisfied with forty thousand marks?

AUGUSTE. (*Nudging her father*) Say yes, quick —or he'll come down again.

HEINECKE. I can't believe it, Herr Councillor! Even the forty—There isn't that much money—It's nonsense—show me the money.

MUHLINGK. It is at the office, waiting for you.

HEINECKE. And the cashier won't say: Put the fellow out—he's drunk!—Oh, he can be right sharp with the poor people when he wants to—that cashier! (MUHLINGK *draws out a check and fills it; hands it to* HEINECKE: *they all study the writing*) Forty thousand marks! Always the generous gentleman, Herr Councillor. Give me your hand!

MUHLINGK. (*Putting his hand in his pocket*) One thing more: to-morrow evening a moving van will be in front of your door; within two hours you will be good enough to leave my property,—and I hope that will be the last I hear of you.

HEINECKE. Don't say that, Herr Councillor! If the visit of an honest old man isn't disagreeable to you, I'll take the liberty of calling now and then. Yes, I'm an honest old man!

MUHLINGK. Certainly! Good-day, my good people! (*Aside*) Pah! (*He goes out*)

HEINECKE. Mother! Forty thousand! (MICHALSKI *tries to embrace him*) Three paces to the rear, my son! (*Takes out an old handkerchief and carefully does up the check in it, then puts it in breast pocket*) Now you can be as tender as you like.

FRAU HEINECKE. I'm half sick with joy! (*The two embrace and weep*) When I think! I don't

need to go to market without money any more. And
when I'm cold in the afternoons, I can make a fire
without having a bad conscience—a good fire—and
in the evening cold meat!

HEINECKE. And in the evening I can take the
horse-car whenever I want!

MICHALSKI. Exactly four hundred thousand
times, at ten pfennigs per!

FRAU HEINECKE. And you'll buy me a sofa.

AUGUSTE. Now you won't be going to India.

FRAU HEINECKE. For the Lord's sake.

HEINECKE. Are you crazy?

AUGUSTE. And what will Herr Robert have to
say to that?

FRAU HEINECKE. (*Happily*) Yes—Robert!
(*Goes to bedroom door*)

AUGUSTE. (*Holding her back*) I advise you to
let him sleep. He'll hear about it soon enough.

FRAU HEINECKE. (*Startled*) What d'you mean
by that?

HEINECKE. (*Pulling at* FRAU HEINECKE'S *dress
and pointing to kitchen door*) He! he! Her! In
there!

FRAU HEINECKE. Oh, the poor, dear child!

HEINECKE. (*Mysteriously*) We'll give her a
little surprise!—Shh! (*All tiptoe to the kitchen
door*—HEINECKE, *who is leading the way, opens the
door suddenly, then with a cry, starts back*) Wha—
wh—Mother! What's that?

FRAU HEINECKE. (*Clasping her hands above her
head*) Good Lord!

MICHALSKI. (*Looking over their shoulders*)
The devil!

HEINECKE. (*With pretended severity*) You
come here!

ALMA. (*Outside*) Oh, please—no!

HEINECKE. Are you coming?

(*Enter* ALMA *dressed in the robe of the Indian*

*Princess, her hands covering her face for
shame. All laugh and exclaim in surprise at
the costume.* AUGUSTE *feels the material.*)

AUGUSTE.   The Indian dress.
MICHALSKI.   From the stark-naked princess!
ALMA.   I—just—wanted—to try it on! I'll take
it right off!
FRAU HEINECKE.   Ach! what a little angel!
ALMA.   Aren't you angry with me any more?
HEINECKE.   Angry!   (*Then recalling his se-
verity*)   That is—yes—very. But for once we'll
allow mercy to take the place of justice. (*Turning
around*)   That was pretty good, eh?
FRAU HEINECKE.   (*Strokes* ALMA'S *hair and
leads her toward the left*) Come, sit down. No,
here on the arm-chair!
ALMA.   What is it—what's happened?
HEINECKE.   Ha! ha!

(ALL *take their places about him.*)

ALMA.   And I can go to the masked ball?
HEINECKE.   Ha—ha! Yes, you can go to the
masked ball.
AUGUSTE.   (*Ironically*) The poor child!
HEINECKE.   (*Jumping up*)   I must go this minute to the bank!
MICHALSKI.   (*Opening bottle of liqueur*) Wait!
We'll wet up our luck so it'll stick! Alma, some
glasses.
FRAU HEINECKE.   (*Getting up*) Let the poor
child sit still! I'll 'tend to that myself! (*She goes
to the washstand and brings a set of liqueur
glasses. To* AUGUSTE) What did you mean before
about Robert?
AUGUSTE.   You'll see quick enough.
FRAU HEINECKE.   He won't grudge us old folks
a little good luck, will he?

MICHALSKI. (*Sings*) "*So leben wir, so leben wir!*"

(*The moving of a chair is heard in bedroom.*)

MICHALSKI. Ladies and Gentlemen, I drink to Fraulein Alma Heinecke, our lucky-child, and above all, the House that has always shown itself. generous——
HEINECKE. The house of Muhlingk! Long live the House of Muhlingk! Hurrah!

(ROBERT *appears at the bedroom door.*)

ALL. Hurrah! Hurrah!
FRAU HEINECKE. (*Startled*) There he is!

(*Embarrassed silence.*)

MICHALSKI. Morning, brother-in-law.
ROBERT. Will you kindly explain, Mother, how these two happen to be sitting at the table of respectable people?
MICHALSKI. Oh!
HEINECKE. Don't be so inhospitable!
FRAU HEINECKE. (*Going toward him*) Bobby, you mustn't be proud, specially to your own flesh and blood.
ROBERT. Hm—Alma, what is that? Who gave you permission——?
HEINECKE. And you may as well know now as any time, there's no use having any hopes about India. I prefer to spend my money in Germany.
ROBERT. (*Confused*) What has happened?
FRAU HEINECKE. You tell him, Father, you're the one that got the check!
ROBERT. What check?
HEINECKE. (*Assuming a pose*) My son!—one doesn't often seem what one really is—Such things

are deeper—For that reason one must always be respectful—you can never tell what is hidden under
tattered clothes. Anyone can wear a fur-lined coat.

ROBERT. Will you please explain what——

HEINECKE. Explain?—What is there to explain
—Don't look at me like that! What are you looking
at me that way for, Mother. I won't stand it!

FRAU HEINECKE. Go on! Go on!

HEINECKE. Well, as I said, it's simple enough.
The Herr Councillor was here.

ROBERT. He? Why didn't you call me.

HEINECKE. Ah—In the first place because it was
not the young Muhlingk—When *your* friend comes,
then you can receive him. The old gentleman is my
friend—We've promised to call on each other. And
second: because I don't have to ask my son what is
right for me to do—Now you know—See?

FRAU HEINECKE. Oh, Father!

HEINECKE. Don't interrupt me when I'm giving
my son a little admonition. From now on I'm not
going to be fooled with.

MICHALSKI. (*Behind him*) That's the way to
talk.

ROBERT. Was the discussion about Alma?

HEINECKE. In the first place the discussion was
about you. You have been discharged from his
service, because of insubordination. Frankly, I expected more gratitude.

ROBERT. You?

HEINECKE. (*Sternly*) Yes, me! Your honest
old father!—It isn't pleasant for me to have my son
wander around as a clerk out of a job. Now you've
got till four to settle your accounts or it will go
hard with you.

ROBERT. (*About to break out—controls himself*)
Let's talk about Alma! Did he offer satisfaction?

HEINECKE. Certainly, absolute.

ROBERT. (*Hesitating, as if saying something
foolish*) Ah—marriage?

HEINECKE. What marriage?

ROBERT. With his son——

HEINECKE. You must be crazy.

ROBERT. (*Anxiously*) Well, what else?

HEINECKE. (*Slyly in his ear*) Forty thousand marks! (*Aloud*) Fine, eh?

ROBERT. (*With a cry*) Money!

FRAU HEINECKE. (*Frightened*) Lord! I thought so!

HEINECKE. Yes, sir! Here it is, good as gold!

ROBERT. What! you took it?

HEINECKE. (*Wonderingly*) Well?

ROBERT. He offered you money and you took it! (*Against his will he springs toward his father*)

MICHALSKI. (*Stepping between them*) I advise you to leave the old man alone!

ROBERT. (*Reeling back without notcing him*) Mother, you took it!

FRAU HEINECKE. (*Folding her hands*) We're poor folks, my boy! (ROBERT *sinks down with a strange laugh on the work-stool.* MICHALSKI *and* AUGUSTE *gather about* HEINECKE *and* FRAU HEINECKE; ALMA *sits smiling, with folded hands*) God have mercy on us! There's something wrong with him! (*Puts her hand on his shoulder*) My Boy, take a little advice from your poor old mother. Don't step on your good fortune's toes, for pride dies on the straw.

ROBERT. Straw wouldn't be the worst, Mother— I shall die on the grave's edge, or in the gutter like a street cur! Only do give the money back—(*Desperately*) See, I am talking perfectly calmly, perfectly sensibly, I'll show you as plain as day what you must do. That fellow has brought us into disgrace—But we are innocent—We needn't be ashamed before anyone. A man can steal honor just the same as he can steal a purse. No one can prevent that!—But if we let someone buy our honor with cold money, then we have no honor at all—and it serves us right—(HEINECKE *turns to* MICHALSKI, *touching his forehead*) Heaven knows I understand it all! I'm not critcizing—Really I'm not.— You are poor and you've always been poor. Such a miserable existence! Nothing but worry for daily bread destroys all judgment and all dignity. And now you let yourselves be blinded by a little money! —but believe me, it will never give you pleasure. Nothing will be left but disgust! (*Choking*) Ah, the disgust! It chokes——

FRAU HEINECKE. That kind of talk is enough to turn you cold——

HEINECKE. So *that* is my son!

ROBERT. And don't imagine that you will lose by taking my advice. Look at me! I have learned a few things, haven't I? I'm healthy, I can be trusted, can't I—The few remaining years you can trust to me, can't you?—Can't you see. I want nothing better than to work for you—I'll make you rich! Rich! you can do what you like with me! I'll be your slave! Your pack-horse—Only give back that money!

HEINECKE. That's all very well! But a bird in the hand—Let me tell you!

MICHALSKI. You're right there, Father!

HEINECKE. I certainly am right!—You run along and chase your sparrows, my boy. I'll keep the bird I've got.

MICHALSKI. Bravo!

ROBERT. And you, Mother?—(*She turns away*) You too?—God, what have I left?—Alma, what about you? I offer you everything. Only help me! (*He takes her hand. She struggles a little. He draws her toward the center*) You've given yourself away. Well, perhaps that's your right. But you won't *sell* yourself—you can't sell your love in the public market. Alma, tell them that!

ALMA. (*Angrily*) Let me go!

AUGUSTE. He's breaking the kid's arm.

ALMA. You've got nothing to say to me any more. (*She breaks away*)

ROBERT. Little sister!

ALMA. And I'm going to the masked ball, too! Ask mother if I ain't.

ROBERT. Mother!

FRAU HEINECKE. Why shouldn't the poor child have a little fun once in a while?

ROBERT. (*Overcome*) So we've gone that far?

MICHALSKI. (*Sitting in chair, mockingly*) Yes, we've gone that far!

ROBERT. You—*Procuror!* Get out of that chair! (MICHALSKI *remains seated*, ROBERT *takes hold of the back of the chair*) Get up, I say, and get out of here, both of you!

MICHALSKI. (*Threateningly*) Now that's a little too fresh!

ROBERT. (*Who has seized the chair*) Dare to lay a hand on me!

FRAU HEINECKE. (*Throwing herself between them*) You'll break my arm-chair.

ROBERT. I suppose that comes from our friends on the Avenue whom you hold in such high esteem!

FRAU HEINECKE. Of course it does!

ROBERT. From our dear Herr Kurt, I suppose?

FRAU HEINECKE. Well, yes!

ROBERT. (*With a wild laugh*) There it is, then! (*He throws the chair to the floor, breaking it and kicking the pieces away from him*)

FRAU HEINECKE. (*Weeping*) My beautiful arm-chair! (*She picks up the pieces carrying them to the left—then she sinks down on stool*)

HEINECKE. This is getting uncomfortable! (*He starts to go out, right*)

ROBERT. (*Standing in his way*) Will you give that blood-money back? Yes or no?

HEINECKE. Give it back? (*Contemptuously*) Huh!

ROBERT. Then I'm through with you! and you,

too, Mother. Is a man brought into the world for
that! To wear dishonor like a birthmark? Very
good! If I had to be born, why didn't you leave
me in the dirt when I first saw the day? Where I've
got to wallow for the rest of my life because my
worthy family desires it!

AUGUSTE. Do you hear that, Mother, and he was
always your favorite.

ROBERT. No, no, Mother, don't listen to me!
(Kneeling beside her) I said nothing! If I said
anything, it was only madness. To-day I feel as
though I were cut loose from everything that is
·human—or natural! Mother, have pity on me!
You can save me! Come with me!

FRAU HEINECKE. *(Sobbing)* How do I know
you won't break the mirror, too! in your blind fits.

ROBERT. *(Looks wildly at mirror, then rises)*
We speak different languages—We can't understand each other.

MICHALSKI. *(Who has been quietly talking to*
·HEINECKE. *He slaps* ROBERT *on the shoulder)*
Now you've raised enough hell! Get out of here!

ROBERT. *(Pushing him out of the way)* Back!
(As his parents and sisters surround him with an-
gry cries. Breaks out in hollow laughter) Ah, so
that's it! You throw me out?

MICHALSKI. *(Opens door)* Get out!

(COUNT TRAST *appears on threshold.)*

TRAST. *(Slapping* MICHALSKI *on shoulder)*
Thank you humbly for the friendly welcome!

ROBERT. *(Recognizing* TRAST, *cries out, then ex-*
tends his arms as if to urge him away) What do
·you want here?—In this dive?—Do you know who
we are?—We sell ourselves!—*(He laughs)* Look
·at me! No, I can't bear it! *(He covers his face*
with hands)

(*At the sight of* TRAST, ALMA *shamefacedly slinks
away.* MICHALSKI *and* AUGUSTE *follow her
into kitchen.*)

TRAST. Pull yourself together! What has happened?

HEINECKE. (*Hat in hand*) He acted very undutifully, Count! First he wanted to take us off
to India, now he wants to take our money away.
I'm just going to the bank—Whole forty thousand
marks, Count, I have the honor—(*Bowing*) Count!
(*He goes out*)

TRAST. Yes, I understand. (*Lays his hand on*
ROBERT'S *shoulder*) Was Herr Muhlingk here?

ROBERT. My friend! Thank you—I had forgotten!

TRAST. What is it?

ROBERT. He wants my accounts. He shall have
them. (*Hurries to trunk which he opens and feverishly looks for something*)

FRAU HEINECKE. (*Weeping*) You can thank
the Lord, Count, you're not married! There are
right ungrateful sons in this world!

TRAST. (*To himself*) You talk like a mother—
(*Realizing what he has said*) Pah! Trast, that
wasn't nice!

FRAU HEINECKE. Ain't I right?

TRAST. (*Takes her hands in his*) A mother is
always right. She has suffered and loved too much
to be anything else. (*Shakes her hand*)

FRAU HEINECKE. But, Count! You shake
hands with a poor old woman!

TRAST. I have sinned against the mothers, and
I must beg forgiveness. And my own not the least.
There are worse sons, than yours, my dear woman.

(ROBERT *takes out a leather portfolio, looks through
it, and lays it aside. Then he takes out a revolver which he tests.*)

TRAST. (*Aside*) Ah, a revolver! This is how he's going to settle accounts!

(ROBERT, *seeing he is observed, quickly hides the revolver in his breast pocket. He takes his hat and portfolio and comes forward.*)

ROBERT. Now I'm ready!
TRAST. I'll go with you.
ROBERT. You?
TRAST. Have I the right?
ROBERT. (*Hesitatingly*) Good, come!
FRAU HEINECKE. (*Tenderly, in tears*) Robert!
ROBERT. (*Tries to conceal his excitement*) I—shall come—again—to say—good-bye! Now I have something important to do. (*He goes towards the door*)
FRAU HEINECKE. (*At the door, wringing her hands*) Herr Kurt and him! Oh, there'll be trouble!
TRAST. (*Aside*) Shh! ssh!—Well, are we off?
ROBERT. (*To his mother, in great excitement, tenderly*) And if we—don't see each other—(*Controlling himself*) Good! We'll go!

(*Both go out as*

THE CURTAIN FALLS.)

ACT IV.

SCENE:—*Same as in Act II.*

(TRAST, WILHELM *and* ROBERT *discovered.* ROBERT *carries a portfolio under his arm.*)

WILHELM. (*Aside to* TRAST) I have strict orders not to let Herr Heinecke in.

TRAST. Nor me?

WILHELM. Oh, with the Count it is a different matter.

TRAST. Thank you for the trust you put in me. Herr Heinecke is accompanied by me. I shall be responsible for his prsence here. We shall wait for the Herr Councillor.

WILHELM. But——

TRAST. Which do you prefer—specie or paper? (*Looking for money in his pocket-book*) Is the whole house empty?

WILHELM. The Herr Councillor has gone to the factory, the Gnadige Frau has a headache, the Gnadiges Fraulein has gone to the city—Herr Kurt likewise.

TRAST. Together?

WILHELM. Oh, they never go together—Herr Kurt wanted to countermand the invitation—because—(*Indicates* ROBERT)

TRAST. (*Gives him money*) Good! That's all!

WILHELM. Nothing further, sir?

TRAST. Go.

(WILHELM *bows and goes out*)

Come here, my boy.

ROBERT. What do you want?

TRAST. What do I want? You know I never

want anything. These things don't affect me. But the question is: What do *you* want here—in this house?

ROBERT. I want to settle my account.

TRAST. Of course—we know that—But, inasmuch as you are willing to forego the generous handshake that the workman usually gets at this proud moment, I should think you would send the accounts to the office—and—(*With gesture of finality*)

ROBERT. That would be simple enough.

TRAST. My dear man, let me talk to you as a friend!

ROBERT. Go ahead, talk!

TRAST. You are pursuing a phantom!

ROBERT. Really?

TRAST. No one has touched your honor.

ROBERT. Really!

TRAST. Because nobody in the world could do it.

ROBERT. Really, really!

TRAST. This thing that you call honor—this mixture of shame, and "tempo," and—honesty and pride, things you have acquired through a civilized existence and as a result of your own loyalty, why this can no more be taken away from you by a piece of treachery than your generosity or your judgment! Either it is a part of yourself or else it doesn't exist at all. The sort of honor that can be destroyed by a blow from a fop's glove has nothing to do with you! That is nothing but a mirror for the dandies, a plaything for the indolent and a perfume to the boulevardier.

ROBERT. You talk like someone trying to make a virtue out of necessity.

TRAST. Perhaps—because every virtue is a direct result of necessity.

ROBERT. And my family?

TRAST. I didn't think you had a family now! (ROBERT *buries his face in his hands*). I understand—it's a contraction of the nerves after the limb is amputated.—Don't deceive yourself! Even though the foot still pains you, the leg is gone!

ROBERT. You never had a sister!

TRAST. —Tell me, must I, the aristocrat, learn what abasement means from you, a plebeian? My boy, don't forswear your parents. Don't say that they are worse than you or I.—They are different, that's all. Their sensations are sensations that are strange to you, the point of view they hold is simply beyond your comprehension. Therefore to criticize them is not only narrow-minded, but presumptuous—And you may as well know soon as late: in your struggle with your people you have been wrong from beginning to end!

ROBERT. Trast, you say that!

TRAST. I take the liberty—You come back from a foreign country where you have been associating with triple-plated gentlemen, and then you expect your people, in order to please you, to change the very skins they live in; although they've fitted perfectly all these years! That is immodest, my boy! And your sister has really received back her honor from the family Muhlingk; the honor which she can make use of. For everything on this earth has its price and value. The honor of the Avenue may be paid for with blood—may be, I said. The honor of the Alley is restituted with a little capital, *in integrum*. (*As* ROBERT *steps towards him angrily*) Don't eat me up! I haven't finished! Yes—what other significance has a girl's honor—and that's what we're concerned with now—than to bring a sort of dowry of pure-heartedness and honesty to her husband. She is there for one purpose and that is marriage! Just be so good as to make a few inquiries in the society from which you come and see if your sister, with the money that has dropped into her lap, can't make a much better match than she otherwise could!

Robert. Trast, you are cruel, you are crude!

Trast. Crude like Nature, cruel like Truth! Only the indolent and the cowardly surround themselves *a tout prix* with idyllics—But you have nothing to do with them now. Come, give me your hand, shake the dust of home off your feet and don't look back!

Robert. First I must have personal satisfaction.

Trast. So you insist on fighting a duel with him?

Robert. Yes.

Trast. Don't be so old-fashioned.

Robert. Old-fashioned—I may be. Perhaps because I came into the world as a plebeian and because my conception of honor was acquired. I haven't the strength to rise to the heights of your standpoint. Let me go down in my own narrowness if I must.

Trast. But suppose he won't give satisfaction?

Robert. I shall find some way to force him.

Trast. Aha! (*Aside*) the revolver!—One thing more, my boy; if you have made up your mind to let Herr Kurt put a bullet through you, you must take away every pretext for his refusing.

Robert. Heavens, yes! you are right!

Trast. (*Drawing out his pocket-book*) Does that embarrass you?

Robert. No, you have done too much for me, for me to ask——

Trast. (*Filling out a check*) There!

Robert. And if I can never pay that back?

Trast. Then I'll write it in the largest ledger, where the accounts of friendships are kept. (*Stroking his head*) It won't be as bad as that! Hm—my boy—one thing you've forgotten.

Robert. What?

Trast. Leonore.

Robert. (*Shuddering*) Don't speak of her!

Trast. You love her.

ROBERT. Oh!—I shan't answer!

TRAST. Would you like to have her think of you as the murderer of her brother.

ROBERT. Better than if she had to think of me as a man without honor.

TRAST. (*Straightening up*) Am I not a so-called " man without honor?" And haven't you found me a good fellow? And don't I carry my head as high as anyone in the world? Shame on you!

ROBERT. (*After a pause*) Trast—forgive me!

TRAST. Forgive—Nonsense, I like you!—That's enough!

ROBERT. Trast—I—won't fight—the duel!

TRAST. Your word?

ROBERT. My word!

TRAST. Come, then.

ROBERT. Where?

TRAST. How do I know? Into the world.

ROBERT. Forgive me—shall I?

(*Enter* WILHELM.)

WILHELM. The Herr Councillor has just come into his office.

TRAST. (*Aside*) Kurt not home!—That's good.

ROBERT. I'll go in. (*He takes his portfolio*)

TRAST. Good! Wait for me!

ROBERT. What do you want here?

TRAST. Never mind about that. Come here. (*Aside to* ROBERT) Before you go, give me your revolver.

ROBERT. (*Startled*) You know?

TRAST. Anyone could see it inside your coat.

ROBERT. Please—let me keep it—or can't you trust me?

TRAST. I'm afraid that story of Pepe will go to your head.

ROBERT. Hasn't a word of honor between two dishonored men any value?

TRAST. Good! Keep it. (ROBERT *goes out followed by* WILHELM. TRAST *is about to follow him, but stops*)—Perhaps it was imprudent after all?—But if the youngster comes home, I'll keep them apart. Now there is something else to attend to. If this girl here is what I think she is—(*Enter* LEONORE L. *wearing a winter costume*) Ah, this is very fortunate.

LEONORE. (*Giving him her hand. Excitedly*) Count, do you know where I've been? To your apartment! (*Takes her coat and hat off*) Are you shocked at my boldness? But you were the only one to whom I could go to find out what has happened. I was afraid my brother was on the way to ruin that young girl. I suspected it. Has your friend found out?

TRAST. If that were all!

LEONORE. What else could there be——

TRAST. I admit, I really can't find words to——

LEONORE. Please tell me!

TRAST. Very well! Your parents have considered it necessary to make those poor people forget their trouble—so they appealed to them on their weakest side—namely, by their poverty.

LEONORE. Do you mean to say that?—that—they —*bought* my brother's—(*As* TRAST *nods*) Oh, God!

TRAST. It goes without saying that personally I offer no criticism of them whatever. That is the customary means of ending such relationships. But I am afraid for my friend.

LEONORE. (*Her face in her hands*) How can I ever make it up to him?

TRAST. Do you feel that it is your duty?

LEONORE. My duty? My whole being revolts against this disgusting practice of my home!—Pay! —always pay! pay for honor, pay for love, pay for justice! We can afford it, we have the money.

(*Throws herself into a chair. Then springing up*)
Forgive me! I don't know what I'm doing! I
spoke of my family as though they were strangers.

TRAST. Perhaps they are more strangers to you
than you think!

LEONORE. (*Confused*) If you were only right!
(*As he appears to listen to something outside*)
What is it?

TRAST. Isn't that your brother's voice?

LEONORE. (*At the door*) Yes, with some of his
friends.

TRAST. (*Aside*) I shouldn't have let him keep
the revolver. (*Taking his hat*) Is he going to the
office?

LEONORE. No, I think they are coming here.

TRAST. (*Putting his hat down again*) Good, I
will wait for him—One thing, Fraulein—My friend
leaves this house to-day; he leaves the city to-morrow and perhaps Europe in a short time.

LEONORE. (*To herself*) Oh, God!

TRAST. But to-day I should like to prevent a
meeting between him and your brother. If that
meeting does occur, without my being able to prevent it, I should like you to remain in the vicinity.

LEONORE. (*She nods; voices are heard at the
door. She hurries to the left, then turns*) What
shall I do, Count?

TRAST. Be true to him!

LEONORE. I will! (*She goes*)

TRAST. Now—the brother!

(*Enter* KURT, LOTHAR *and* HUGO.)

KURT. (*Surprised*) Count!

LOTHAR. (*Aside*) Good thing we came with
you!

TRAST. I should like a few words with you, Herr
Muhlingk.

KURT. Sorry, but I am very pressed for time; my father is waiting for me!

TRAST. (*Aside*) Oho!—(*To* KURT) It's a personal favor.

KURT. I have no secrets from my friends, Count. (*They sit down*)

TRAST. Someone, a great friend of mine, has suffered deeply because of his honor. On my advice and as a favor to me he has foregone sending you a challenge.

KURT. You are mistaken, Count; Herr Heinecke received satisfaction.

LOTHAR. We could allow no other satisfaction.

TRAST. (*Looks at him from head to foot*) We won't go into that any further, Herr Muhlingk. My friend at this moment is with your father, settling his accounts in person.

KURT. Well, that is his privilege.

TRAST. He is to have an interview with him at the same time.

KURT. That is also his privilege, Count.

TRAST. In an hour my friend will have left this establishment. In consideration of the strain of excitement under which he is probably suffering at present, it would be to the advantage of both sides if a meeting between you could be avoided.

LOTHAR. That——

TRAST. (*Quietly*) Herr Lieutenant, I have not as yet taken the liberty of addressing you! Herr Muhlingk, let us consider this seriously. You are speaking with some one who has your material welfare at heart—not out of sympathy, I am free to admit—Therefore, I may speak to you almost as a friend, don't let these gentlemen intimidate you.

HUGO. No, don't let us intimidate you!

TRAST. And consider this! I don't dare think of the wrong I have done that man—you will—you'll do me this favor?

LOTHAR. (*Behind* KURT) Now show him!

KURT. I have nothing to say, Count, because I find it impossible to choose words to express my astonishment at your extraordinary request.

(All rise.)

LOTHAR. *(To* KURT, *aside)* Fine! fine!

KURT. And furthermore, I should like to know by what right you dare make such a request to me in my own house?

TRAST. You refuse?

KURT. Do you still doubt it, Count?

LOTHAR. *(Aside to him)* More cutting, more cutting.

TRAST. *(Aside)* Force—Yes, I doubted it, for I still cherished the slight hope that I was dealing with a man of honor—I beg your pardon—I made a mistake.

KURT. Sir—that is——

TRAST. An insult—yes.

KURT. Which will be properly dealt with.

TRAST. I ask for nothing better.

KURT. You will hear from me to-morrow.

TRAST. To-morrow—So you sleep on a thing like that? I am accustomed to settling such matters at once.

KURT. *(Chokingly)* Immediately.

TRAST. *(Aside)* Thank God! *(Aloud)* Then we'll go!

LOTHAR. *(Stepping between)* Always correct, Kurt. You, as principal, have nothing further to do with the gentleman. *(Sharply)* In the first place, Count, the Code of Honor permits the challenged as well as the challenger twenty-four hours in which to arrange his affairs. We, my principal and I—shall make use of this rule, unless—and now I come to the second point—we shall be prevented from enjoying that privilege—for you, Sir, have not insulted us——

TRAST. Ah!

LOTHAR. You belong to those who *cannot* insult us.

TRAST. (*Merrily*) Ah, yes!

LOTHAR. Will you be kind enough to recall, that the Count von Trast-Saarberg, as we can still see in the register,—on the twenty-fifth of June, 1864, was released, under a cloud, from his regiment, because of unpaid gambling debts. That is all. (*Bows negligently*)

TRAST. (*Breaking out into laughter*) Gentlemen, I thank you heartily for the little lesson—I certainly deserved it—for the worst crime under heaven is to be illogical! And one thing I see above everything else. No matter how much a man is elevated above the modern Honor he must still remain her slave, even if it is only when he wants to help a poor devil of a friend out of a hole—Gentlemen, I have the honor—Pardon! I *haven't* the honor! You have denied me that; so nothing remains but the pleasure—the pleasure of saying "Good-day," but that is better still! (*He goes out laughing*)

HUGO. Here we are with our honor and still we've made ourselves ridiculous.

LOTHAR. We acted quite correctly.

HUGO. But, Lothar, the coffee, the coffee.

LOTHAR. One must be willing to sacrifice for the sake of his Honor, my friend. I am glad I could do you this service, Kurt—What would you have done without me? Well, until to-night.

KURT. Are you going back to town already?

LOTHAR. Yes.

KURT. I'll go with you.

LOTHAR. Oh, that will look as though you wanted to get away from the noble brother.

KURT. What do you mean?

LOTHAR. Do you want the Count to laugh in his sleeve? Now it has become almost a duty to stay.

KURT. Hardly that.

LOTHAR. Your duty, unless you want it thought you are a coward.

(*Enter* MUHLINGK *in a fur coat and hat,* WILHELM *follows him.*)

MUHLINGK. (*Throwing his coat to* WILHELM) What is that fellow thinking of to try and get into my office?—Good-day, gentlemen—let him send the books to me, then tell him to go to the devil—(WILHELM *leaves*) Kurt, why are you sneaking away? We've got a little bone to pick, eh?

KURT. (*Aside to his friends*) Now I'm in for it—Get out now! before the storm!

HUGO. Herr Councillor, we haven't much time——

MUHLINGK. Good-day, gentlemen, I regret exceedingly. Good-day.

LOTHAR. (*Aside*) You tell us how the thing comes out.

(LOTHAR *and* HUGO *go out.*)

MUHLINGK. This time I've cleaned the matter up satisfactorily, and the sacrifice, God knows, will be put down to your debit. Now for the moral side of the question.

(*Enter* FRAU MUHLINGK.)

KURT. (*Aside*) Here comes the old lady, this will be great.

FRAU MUHLINGK. Oh, Kurt! Kurt!

KURT. Yes, Mother?

FRAU MUHLINGK. (*Sitting*) You have brought a great deal of trouble to your parents. You forced your father to bargain with that rabble. (LEONORE *enters left*) Oh, how disgusting! what humiliation for us! (*To* LEONORE) What do you want?

LEONORE. I have something to say to you.

MUHLINGK. We haven't time now, go to your room.

LEONORE. No, Father. I can't play the part of the silent daughter any longer. If I am a member of the family I want to take part in this conversation.

MUHLINGK. What is the meaning of all this ceremony?

LEONORE. Something very unfortunate has taken place in our family.

MUHLINGK. I don't know anything——!

LEONORE. You needn't try to hide it from me. According to the rules of modern hypocrisy which are applied to the so-called young ladies, I ought to go about with downcast eyes and play the part of innocent ignorance. Under the circumstances that doesn't work. I have heard about the whole affair.

FRAU MUHLINGK. And you aren't ashamed of yourself?

LEONORE. (*Bitterly*) I am ashamed of myself.

MUHLINGK. Do you know whom you are speaking to? Are you mad?

LEONORE. If my tone was impertinent, please forgive me. I want to soften you, not to quarrel with you. Perhaps I have been a bad daughter— Perhaps I really haven't the right to have my own thoughts as long as I do not eat my own bread—If that is true, try to pardon me—I will make up for it a thousand times. But understand—give him back his honor——

MUHLINGK. I won't ask you again what the fellow is to you?—what do you mean by " giving him back his honor? "

LEONORE. Heavens, you must first at least have the good will to make up for what has happened. Then we can find the means later.

MUHLINGK. You think so? Sit down, my child —I shall let my customary mildness still govern me and try to bring you to reason, although perhaps a stricter method would be more in place—Look at this old gray head. A great deal of honor has been piled up there and still in my whole life I have never meddled with this so-called sense of honor—ah, what a person has to endure without even saying " Hum " when he expects to succeed in life. Here is a young man from whom you say, I have taken his honor. Taking for granted that you are right— where does a young fellow like that get his honor? From his family? Or from my business? My clerks are no knights. You say he had honor, and I'm supposed to give it back to him. How? By taking his sister as a daughter-in-law?

FRAU MUHLINGK. Really, Theodore, you mustn't say these things even as a joke.

MUHLINGK. If I did that, I should disgrace myself and my family. On the other hand, this young man has the chance of getting out of the trouble. If he refuses, and it comes back to me, who shall be made unhappy, we or he? My answer is: he shall, I have no desire to be, myself—That's the way I've always done, and everyone knows me as a man of honor.

LEONORE. (*Rising*) Father, is that your last word?

MUHLINGK. My last! Now, come, give me a kiss and beg your mother's pardon.

LEONORE. (*Shrinks back with a shudder*) Let me go! I can't deceive you!

MUHLINGK. What do you mean?

LEONORE. Father, I feel I am in the wrong, that I am asking the impossible from you. I shall have to know the world differently from—(*Stops suddenly and listens. There are voices in the hall*)

MUHLINGK. And——?

LEONORE. (*Aside*) It's he!—Oh, I can't stand it any longer!

(*Enter* WILHELM.)

WILHELM. The young Herr Heinecke from the Alley is there again.

(KURT *starts.*)

MUHLINGK. Did you tell him what I told you to say?

WILHELM. Yes, Herr Councillor, but he followed me here from the office.

MUHLINGK. What impertinence!—If he doesn't leave this——!

KURT. Pardon me, Father. Perhaps he only wants to thank you! I believe he has reasons.

MUHLINGK. Such people never give you thanks.

KURT. Has he money to give you?

MUHLINGK. Certainly.

KURT. There must be something back of it— get it over and we'll be done with him.

MUHLINGK. As far as I'm concerned—let him come.

(WILHELM *goes out.*)

FRAU MUHLINGK. We'll go, Leonore.

LEONORE. (*Aside*) Kurt!

KURT. Well?

LEONORE. Be on your guard!

KURT. Bah! (*Trying to hide his fear*)

(FRAU MUHLINGK *and* LEONORE *go out. Enter* ROBERT, *apparently calm, respectful in manner —he carries a portfolio.*)

MUHLINGK. You were a little insistant, young man—Well, I never criticize a man in the discharge of duty; least of all when he is about to leave his employer, at the eleventh hour. Take a seat!

ROBERT. If you don't mind, I'll remain standing.

MUHLINGK. Just as you like—I had word from

my nephew yesterday. He is getting on well—having a good time—a little too much according to Count Trast—Well, a little pleasure is always in the blood of gentlemen of good family—You have brought the annual report with you, I hope?

ROBERT. Yes.

MUHLINGK. And——

ROBERT. (*To* MUHLINGK) There, sir. (*Takes a sheet and hands it to the* COUNCILLOR)

KURT. (*Playing the part of indifference*) May I see, Father?

MUHLINGK. Yes, yes—or perhaps you have a copy?

ROBERT. Yes, I have.

MUHLINGK. Please give it to my son. (ROBERT *hands it to* KURT. *The two stand, measuring each other with their eyes*) As far as I can see at the first glance that is exceedingly good. The net gain is——

ROBERT. 116,227 Gulden.

MUHLINGK. The dutch gulden is one mark seventy—Kurt figure it with me.

ROBERT. 197,585 Marks.

MUHLINGK. 8—1—3—5—8. Right—197,285 Marks and 90 Pfennigs. Kurt, are you figuring it up?

KURT. And ninety pfennig. Yes, Father.

MUHLINGK. Ha—And in the coffee "a small profit?" What does that mean?

ROBERT. (*Handing him a sheet*) Here is the special account. I was in a position to foresee the crisis caused by the competition in Brazil and I had five-sixths of the area planted with tea.

MUHLINGK. You?

ROBERT. Yes, Herr Councillor, I——

KURT. Strange!

MUHLINGK. And how is the " Quinquina? "

ROBERT. Here is the report. (*Hands him the paper*)

sitting as though dumb) And a new honor! (*He takes her in his arms*)

FRAU MUHLINGK. So that is our thanks, Father!

LEONORE. Father, Mother, I ask your forgiveness, but what I am doing now I must do! I am sure that it can't be wrong. But I beg of you, think kindly of me—sometimes.

MUHLINGK. Ah, and you think you'll leave my house without my curse! (*He lifts his arm as though to curse her*) You——

TRAST. (*Stepping up to him*) No, Herr Councillor, what's the use of wearing yourself out with curses? (*Quietly*) and furthermore, in confidence, your daughter isn't making a bad match. The young fellow will have my station and, since I have no heirs, my fortune.

MUHLINGK. But, Count—why didn't you explain!

TRAST. (*Quickly stepping back and raising his hand as if to bless him*) Please submit your worthy blessing in writing!

(*Follows the two to the door as*

THE CURTAIN FALLS.)

CPSIA information can be obtained
at www.ICGtesting.com
Printed in the USA
BVHW071337231118
533754BV00029B/2950/P